BANKING

AN ILLUSTRATED HISTORY

BANKING

AN ILLUSTRATED HISTORY

EDWIN GREEN

RIZZOLI
NEW YORK

Library of Congress cataloging-in-Publication Data

Green, Edwin.
    A history of banking / Edwin Green.
        p.   cm.
    Bibliography: p.
    Includes index.
    ISBN 0-8474-1072-0
    1. Banks and banking——History.   I. Title.
HG1551.G74   1989
332.1'09——dc19   88-35088 CIP

Printed in West Germany by Mohndruck Graphische Betriebe GmbH, Gütersloh

Captions to illustrations:

Half-title: An exchange banker in early sixteenth century Germany, from a woodcut by Hans Burgkmair (1473–1531). The counter, laden with baskets of coin, could be secured by locking the screen gates – the prototypes of modern counter grilles.

Half-title verso: The Galerie Dorée in the Hotel de Toulouse, Paris, now occupied by the Banque de France. The original interior was designed by Francois Mansart in the early seventeenth century, with eighteenth century additions.

Title-page: *The Banker and his Wife* by Marinus Van Roejmerswaelen (1493–1567). This oil painting of 1538 focuses on the weighing of coin and auditing of accounts in a Flemish counting house.

Pages 6–7: The covered plaza of Southeast Financial, Miami, Florida, USA, designed by S.O.M. of San Francisco. In the 1970s and 1980s the treatment of public space became an essential and often controversial part of architects' briefs for bank development.

Acknowledgements

Key: t top, b bottom, r right, l left

Alexander Turnbull Library, Wellington, New Zealand: p. 80. Amsterdams Historisch Museum: p. 35. Peter Aprahamian: pp. 2; 37; 38; 39; 52; 68; 86; 90; 98; 98–9; 103; 106; 110–111; 118; 158. Arcaid, London: p. 146–7. Australia and New Zealand Banking Group Archive, Melbourne: p. 77. The Governor and Company of the Bank of England, London: pp. 41; 42; 48; 50; 51; 59. Bank of Scotland, Edinburgh: p. 45. Barclays Bank plc, London: pp. 2; 49; 52; 88. The Directors of Barings, London: p. 58. Bridgeman Art Library, London: pp. 3; 19; 30; 43; 63. City of Bristol Museum and Art Gallery: p. 66. Trustees of the British Museum: p. 46. British Library: p. 14; 28tl. Chartered Institute of Bankers, London: p. 68. Chase Manhattan Corporation, New York: pp. 132, 133. Coutts and Co., London: p. 74. Culver Pictures Inc., New York: pp. 81t; 84b; 89. Darblay, Jérôme: p. 54; 119. Esto Photographic, New York: pp. 6–7; 130–1. Euromoney Magazine, London: pp. 8; 112; 124b; 127; 144t. Financial Times Photography: pp. 140–41. Mary Evans Picture Library, London: pp. 20r; 24–25; 75; 76; 94; 95. Mark Fiennes, London: p. 91. Financial Times, London: p. 148. Fondazione Querini Stampalia, Venice: p. 34. Fotomas Index, London: p. 17; 53. Susan Griggs Agency, London: pp. 136r; 159. Worshipful Company of Goldsmiths: p. 36. Guildhall Library, London: p. 63 (photo Bridgeman Art Library). Sonia Halliday/Laura Lushington, Weston Turville: pp. 26; 27. Peter Heman, Zurich: p. 129. The Hongkong and Shanghai Banking Corporation, Hong Kong: pp. 79; 82; 83. Hulton Picture Company, London: pp. 92; 97t; 104; 108; 116; 117; 125. Timothy Hursley, Little Rock, Arkansas: pp. 138; 139; 142; 143; 150; 151; 154–5. Image Bank, London: p. 135. Andrew Lawson, Charlbury: p. 136l. Billy Love Collection, London: p. 78t. Lloyd's Bank plc, London: pp. 44, 100; 101; 105; 115. Mansell Collection, London: pp. 1; 21; 57; 69t; 69b; 96. Mellon Bank, New York: p. 109. The Mercers' Company and National Portrait Gallery, London: p. 28. Midland Bank plc, London: pp. 71; 106; 107; 128b; 158. Monte dei Paschi, Siena: p. 22. National Westminster Bank, plc: pp. 47 (*photo: Bromhead, Ltd., Bristol*); 49; 67; 70; 106. Peter Newark's Historical Pictures: pp. 40; 56; 60; 65; 81bl, br; 84t; 85; 103; 113; 114. Noordbrabants Museum, 's-Hertogenbosch: p. 10. Private Collection, London: p. 62. Roger-Viollet, Paris: pp. 20l; 72. Royal Bank of Scotland, London: pp. 37; 148. Scala, Florence: pp. 15; 23. Schweizerische Bankgesellschaft, Photoarchiv, Zurich: p. 102. Société Générale, Paris: p. 97b. Frank Spooner Pictures, London: pp. 124t; 126; 128t. Ezra Stoller: p. 134. Studio Ivan Nemec, Frankfurt: p. 122. Zefra/Orion, London: p. 78. This project would have been quite impossible without the help and support of Hilary Green, Julie Mehta, Neil Drury and Isobel Gillan. I am also very grateful to my colleagues in banks and bank archives throughout the world, both in locating illustrations and in giving permission for location photographs.

CONTENTS

INTRODUCTION

Few business activities have such a pervasive, across-the-board influence on modern life as banking. The customers of banks include not only private individuals, firms and companies but also nation-states and international organizations. These customers, whether in making payments, investing or borrowing, use a huge range of bank services from many different species of bank. They may be settling a small bill by paying over a banknote, writing a cheque or using a bank credit card; at the other extreme they may be raising multi-billion currency loans for international projects. They may be withdrawing cash from a small branch bank or they may be transmitting enormous and complex payments across the dealing screens of the world's great banking centres. Whatever the scale of the transaction, banking plays a vital and trusted role in contemporary society.

Inevitably an industry with such a permeating influence has produced a vast literature – technical, legal, historical and even sociological. Much of that output has been devoted to the evolution of banking institutions and systems, especially over the last two centuries, and it includes scores of histories of individual banks, biographies and studies of banking events. Yet, apart from histories of banking in particular countries, there have been few general guides to the history of banking in a world-wide setting. As a result, the subject often seems remote or inaccessible to those who are curious to know more of the origins of bank business.

Equally, there is a surprising shortage of illustrated material on the history of banking. At face value banking may not appear to be the most visual of subjects – office routines and solemn meetings are at the forefront of public and media impressions of the industry. Even so, as exhibitions and museums of money and banking around the world can now show, banking has a rich heritage of fine art and design. The banks, yesterday and today, have a distinctive record of patronage of art and architecture. They are also the custodians of remarkable collections of archives and artefacts. Nevertheless, little of this heritage has been presented in accessible published form.

This book has been designed with both of these themes in mind – the need for a short general history of banking, and the presentation of some of the visual riches and curiosities of banking history. In both cases the intention is to set the development of banking in a fully international picture, and to point to the strong economic and social forces at play; to explore the origins and evolution of the main types of banking business; and to show how the banking institutions of the late twentieth century have a long and sometimes complex pedigree. Not least, a general history of banking is the chance to focus upon some of the personalities, dynasties and groups which have left their mark on banking history.

As the pace of change in the contemporary world continues to accelerate, it is all too easy to forget, or to ignore, the long roots of banking business. I hope that this illustrated history will show how the vitality and scale of modern banking has a strong line of development from the enterprise and skills of earlier generations of bankers. These traditions and distinctions surely deserve to be remembered, understood, and celebrated.

Edwin Green
20 April, 1989

The eighteenth-century interior of the Nederlandse Spaarbankbond, Limbourg, the Netherlands.

CHAPTER ONE

MARKETS, MERCHANTS AND PRINCES

Banking from the earliest times to the 16th century

The origins of banking can hardly be pinned down to a precise period or place. In the ancient world coinage, exchange, and lending were treated in a way which had many recognizable features of banking business. From the late twelfth century to the mid-fourteenth century the merchant communities of Italy developed techniques and specializations which are still in the banker's toolbox. The banks of the Renaissance and early modern period are strong contenders as the earliest banking 'institutions' in a modern sense, while the nineteenth century could lay claim to the beginnings of fully professional banking. It may even be said that it was not until the very recent past – especially from the 1960s to the early 1980s – that banking emerged as a 'universal' business in terms of the sheer scale and scope of its modern operations.

The vocabulary of banking gives some clues to the origins of the business. The modern term 'bank' derives from the merchant's bench, or *banco*, in the market-places of medieval Italy. Traders in Lombardy preferred to set up their own dealing benches rather than permanent stalls or shops, but this homely style was not peculiar to money-dealers. Indeed, the 'bench' translation is more useful in tracing the origins of the concept of bankruptcy: the breaking of a merchant's bench in medieval Italy was the signal of his failure. Less literally but more relevantly the words 'bank', *banco* and the German *banck* were synonymous with the Italian *monte*. Meaning a mound or accumulation, the term was used to describe public loans in Venice as early as the twelfth century, and by the fourteenth century the charity loan banks of Italy were known as *monti di pietà* (see p. 22). These public loans and loan banks were no more than a part of the Italian banking scene, however. A clearer view of the origins of banking only emerges by recognizing its continuing, persistent characteristics.

Over the last century and more, definitions of banking have settled upon four key characteristics. To be recognized as a bank by businessmen and lawyers, an institution is expected to receive deposits of money from its customers; to maintain current accounts for them; to provide advances in the form of loans or overdrafts; and to manage payments on behalf of its customers by collecting and paying cheques, bills and other forms of 'banking currency'. In each of these functions a bank is also required to offer security and safe-keeping. As part of that security, a bank must show that its operations enjoy privacy – that banking is not the servant of any other business which it may have taken on. The price of its services will normally be set by the rates of interest, commission, or fees which it charges its customers. These features are common to all categories of banks on the modern financial scene, whether they are 'central' banks with governments as their main customers, commercial and savings banks with their millions of private

View of the market at s'Hertogenbosch, the Netherlands. Fairs and markets were the breeding-ground for new techniques of banking and exchange throughout the Middle Ages and early modern period.

customers, or merchant banks with their select lists of major accounts.

Some of these characteristics were evident in the ancient world. In Mesopotamia lending was available at interest from temples, the royal treasuries and private landowners as long ago as the third millenium BC. In these transactions the lenders – for example the Egibi family of Babylon in the first millenium BC – were deploying their own resources rather than receiving and using others' deposits.

In Greece, even before the appearance of coinage in the seventh century BC, the sanctuary at Delphi was used as a storehouse for bullion and valuables. A similar refuge was created at the temple of Apollo at Didyma near Miletus after the invasions of the Dorians, and later at Olympia. The Athenian economy, developing strongly in the sixth and fifth centuries BC, also produced prototype bankers – individual merchants who would accept deposits of coin and bullion for safe custody, paying out a rate of interest agreed by contract. The attractions of interest income were sufficiently great for Xenophon (c.430–c.356 BC) to propose the formation of a safe-custody institution in which all Athenians could share the profits from interest. This dream, though not realized, foreshadowed mutual and joint-stock ownership of banks.

Elsewhere in the Mediterranean world, the money-changers in the temple of Jerusalem were described in the New Testament as exchanging coins for visiting merchants and also allowing interest on any money deposited with them. In republican and imperial Rome, in contrast to the Greeks' concern with safe-keeping, the emphasis fell upon improving methods of payment. In the second and first centuries BC the State and the patricians of Rome were using money-shops, *tabernae argentariae* or *mensae numulariae*, to deal with tax payments and to settle accounts with their creditors. An assignment or *attributio* could be used as an order to a money-shop to settle payments, in similar fashion to a draft or cheque. The dealers, or *argentarii*, also allowed interest on money lodged, and provided a money-changing service. For the less wealthy citizens of Rome, rudimentary loan banks used the proceeds of property confiscated from criminals to lend money at interest.

It was not until the twelfth and thirteenth centuries, in an Italy of revival and change, that the themes of banking history made a reappearance. On the surface the economic and cultural environment throughout Europe was hostile. The medieval economy remained land-based, dominated by the needs of Church and State. Wealth and income were largely committed to the support of the hierarchical, immobile structure of feudalism in which money, capital and credit played a secondary role to barter and the payment of dues 'in kind'. At the same time the Church was severe in its condemnation of the sin of usury, or 'making money with money'. However, even in the Dark Ages, Jewish merchants had kept alive the trading contacts between the Christian West and the Moslem East, and from the late eleventh to the mid-thirteenth century international trade was given real impetus by the crusades. In return for their financial and military support, the Italian cities of Venice, Genoa and Pisa won privileges throughout the reconquered eastern Mediterranean. The concessions included markets, warehouses and merchant 'quarters' in Constantinople and in the cities of the Egyptian and Levant coasts. The inflow of wealth to Italy brought strong economic growth not only to the great maritime powers but also to the cities inland – Lucca, Siena and Florence in the case of Pisa, Milan and Piacenza in the case of Genoa, and the towns of the Po valley in that of Venice.

The events of this period did not produce a banking tradition by accident or magic. Their real importance in financial history was the creation of *customers* for banking services. On one hand, the kings and princes of Christian Europe could not tackle their crusading adventures without external, international financing, and Italian merchants, especially the Genoese, responded to the challenge with shipments of coin and bullion to the Holy Land in return for credits with the royal treasuries of Europe. In contrast, the wealth sucked into the Italian cities in the age of the crusades itself generated civic and business demands for banking services. In Venice, by the thirteenth century, the international entanglements of the government created a large public debt, financed by its citizens. These creditors 'incorporated' their claims, which enabled citizens to settle their own debts and payments by transferring back and forth their holdings in the public debt.

The business demand for banking services was both stronger and more widely spread than the needs of city-states. In late twelfth-century Genoa, the term *bancherius* was being used to describe money-changers who took deposits and gave credit to local business customers. Similarly in thirteenth-century Venice the *banchi di scritta* transferred payments and accepted deposits from their clients. Italian merchants were also international in their ambitions, particularly in their attendance at the network of trading fairs in northern Europe. From the twelfth century the fairs of Champagne were the most prominent European market-place, serving initially as trade centres for the cloth industries of Flanders and France. Six fairs were held each year – two at Troyes, two at Provins, and one each at both Lagny and Bar-sur-Aube – and they provided an almost continuous cycle of market activity. Merchants from Milan were attending the fairs by the 1170s, soon followed by traders from Piacenza and Lucca.

The special significance of the fairs for the Italian contingent was their role in the settlement of local and international debts. Each fair concluded with a reckoning of debts incurred during the fair, and any debts or credits not settled were carried forward to the next neighbouring fair. This new and liberating system of credit was protected by safe conducts given by the counts of Champagne; it enabled the Italian

merchants to journey to and from the north carrying only a bare minimum of coin specie. In the golden age of the fairs, from the late twelfth century to the end of the thirteenth, the 'Lombards' and the merchants of Paris and Flanders were joined by merchants and money-changers from Germany (especially Cologne), from Barcelona, Rome, Toulouse and the Cahors region. Indeed the dealers of Cahors and Figeac were important enough in the market to become notorious; by the late Middle Ages the term *cahorsin* was synonymous with usury.

By the second half of the thirteenth century the interchange between northern Italy and the fairs of Champagne was producing an identifiable banking industry. Financial specialization was its main feature with private enterprise rather than the demands of the state as its first concern. The merchants from Piacenza and Tuscany who had originally visited the fairs to buy cloth and sell alum and leather now travelled north purely to settle debts and offer exchange to the commodity merchants. In this way the fairs became a financial clearing-house as well as an international trade market. Banking clearances, *giro di partita*, were used to settle complex payments negotiated in other markets. So, for example, in 1257 a merchant from Lucca was able to buy Chinese silk at Genoa, promising that a colleague based in Piacenza would make the payment at the Champagne fairs.

These intermediaries were banking specialists, with their own style of organization and their own techniques. The banking 'firm' or 'company' was already emerging, made up of groups of associates and families who contributed working capital and deposits of cash. Increasingly in the thirteenth century, the heads of these firms remained at their Italian base-camps, leaving much of their dealing and information-gathering at the fairs in the hands of agents. This shift from travelling to 'sedentary' business became even more marked in the next century, when banking firms moved on from agencies to more permanent *branch*

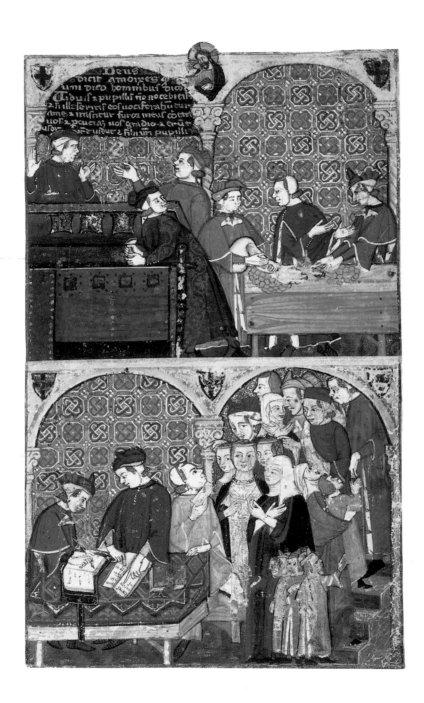

Genoese bankers and their customers dealing in cash and credit, in miniatures from the late fourteenth century manuscript *De Septem Vitiis*. The Genoese had been pioneers of financial techniques since the late twelfth century.

A counting-house in fifteenth century Siena, showing cash payments to the city's officials. The finance of Italian city-states, illustrated here in the *Tablets of the Biccerna* of 1430, was an important proving-ground for techniques of banking and accountancy in the Renaissance period.

representation at home and overseas. The Bardi house of Florence, for example, operated over thirty branches in Italy and overseas with more than 350 personnel. In the early fourteenth century their foreign branches were found as far afield as London, Bruges, Spain, Moorish Africa, and the Levant.

Perhaps the most important technical contribution of these Italian banking houses was their development of bills of exchange for settling payments, particularly in the heavy trading between northern Italy and the fairs of Champagne. Bills of exchange, a vital ingredient of modern banking history, were developed from the 'letters of exchange' used by the Genoese in the late twelfth and thirteenth centuries. In their fourteenth-century form, bills of exchange were written promises to pay a named individual a fixed sum at a near future date. Four individuals or firms participated in the transaction. First, a merchant (A) wished to make a payment to a trader (B) in a distant town or country. A local firm (AA) had an account with a firm (BB) in the relevant town or country. At A's request, AA would therefore write an order (the bill of exchange) to BB, authorizing payment from BB to B. In this fashion A would pay, and B would collect from, their local banking firms.

Delays in the courier services of medieval Europe meant that such transactions were temporary loans as well as payments. Interest could be charged indirectly through the rate of exchange quoted in the bill, avoiding any implication of usury. By the fourteenth century bills of this sort were beginning to serve as the currency of specialist banking firms in western Europe. Their use as a form of payment was to become even more widespread when, from the mid-fifteenth century, merchants and bankers were prepared to trade in bills by buying and selling them at discounted prices. This transition provided the economy of the late medieval period with its own form of banking currency. From the mid-fourteenth century Italian merchants were also using a form of negotiable cheque, the *polizze*, in which orders for payment could be made in writing rather than in person.

If the Italian firms of the late thirteenth century were the first direct ancestors of modern commercial banking, then the financial crises of the fourteenth century deserve to be treated as the predecessors of banking crises of the early modern period. Throughout the Middle Ages there was never any shortage of financial failures. Expulsions of Jewish merchants and the penalization of Lombard traders were almost endemic in thirteenth- and fourteenth-century Europe, ensuring frequent mayhem in the pattern of credit at home and abroad. There were also cases of business failure generated by over-extension, as in the collapse of the house of Buonsignori of Sienna in 1295. More bankruptcies followed in Tuscany in the early fourteenth century. In these cases the failures were local rather than generalized crises, but the transition to widespread financial stress was not delayed for long. Towards the middle of the fourteenth century Florentine houses such as the Bardi, Peruzzi and Acciajoli were in the van of banking development, and their customers included merchants and princes throughout Europe. By the 1330s and 1340s, however, they were committing vast sums in advances to King Edward III of England; the total debt of nearly 1.5 million gold florins was said to be 'worth a kingdom'. Disastrously for the Italian bankers, the debt was created in a territory that was still off the map of financial development. Worse still, Edward III was also rearming at great expense for the campaigns in France which led to the Hundred Years War. Default was inevitable, and the Bardi, Peruzzi and Acciajoli were forced to suspend payments between 1339 and 1343.

The disruption of international finance was immense, reducing the credit of merchants as well as princes. By any standard the suspension of the Florentine firms was a major banking crisis, the first spectacular example of default on a sovereign debt. It

Genoa, from a fifteenth century woodcut. For more than two centuries the Genoese had been in the van of public finance and private banking. Between 1408 and 1444 the city's Banca di San Giorgio was an important experiment in deposit banking.

was also part of the much broader human and economic crisis of the mid-fourteenth century; the arrival of the Black Death in 1347–8 threw most of western and northern Europe into deep shock. The devastation was at its worst in city-ports such as Genoa (where the population of 65,000 was reduced to less than 30,000), Hamburg and Bremen. The economic effects were disastrous, not so much from the shortage of manpower as from the failure of demand.

In spite of these very unpromising conditions, however, banking came into fuller bloom. Florence, hit hard by the stoppage of its premier financial houses, was a long-term victim of the plague. Yet by the early fifteenth century the city could boast the best-designed banking facilities of the pre-modern age. The twin themes of Florence's sophistication were the progress of 'public' banking and the emergence of a formidable tradition of merchant banking. The city of Venice had long ago set a precedent in bringing together government creditors (see p. 13) and Florence itself had incorporated its public debts into a *Monte Commu-*

nale in the thirteenth century. Although the *Monte Communale* was at first a small affair, with assets of less than 50,000 florins in the early fourteenth century, the financial and demographic disasters of the 1340s transformed its role. It now became a refuge of savings for the surviving citizens, lifting total assets from 600,000 florins in the early 1340s to 1.5 million florins in 1364 and 3 million florins by 1400. By the turn of the century between 5,000 and 10,000 citizens were customers of the *Monte*, receiving interest at 5 per cent and transferring holdings between themselves in settlement of trade debts.

This forwardness in public banking was not unique to Florence. In the western Mediterranean a *taula*, in effect a municipal savings bank providing exchange and deposit services, was founded at Barcelona in 1401, and similar units were established at Valencia (1408), Gerona and Saragossa. Genoa, never behind in financial development, gave birth to the remarkable Casa di San Giorgio in 1407. As in Venice and Florence, the Casa brought together the State's creditors in a single fund, and their subscriptions and deposits were 'tradable'. The contributing creditors, as proprietors, also had authority to elect a board of eight directors. From 1408 until 1444 the Banca di San Giorgio – subsidiary to the Casa – also accepted deposits and made loans to officials and to private bankers (see p. 31).

If Florence was an example and a model in public banking, it was even more obviously setting the pace in merchant banking. The Medici bank, Raymond Goldsmith has claimed recently, was:

> . . . 'technically the most advanced financial institution before the late 16th century and possibly the late 17th century and was definitely surpassed in these respects only in the 19th century'.

The Medici family, originally from the Mugello region north of Florence, first came to prominence in the city as merchants and office-holders in the late thirteenth century. A century later they had become a major political and trading clan, and in 1397 they established their own banking house. Under the direction of Cosimo de Medici (1389–1464), the bank achieved real economic and political distinction.

In many respects, Cosimo followed on from and developed the traditions of the Bardi and Peruzzi (one sign of that continuity being his marriage to Contessina Bardi of the old banking family). Like these predecessors and like the other banking houses of Florence, the Medici placed great reliance upon a network of information at home and abroad. Gregorio Dati, a contemporary of Cosimo, observed that the Florentine bankers had 'spread their wings over the world and have information from all its corners'. This network was partly maintained through branch offices; the firm usually operated between six and ten branches in major trading centres such as Venice, Naples, Geneva and Lyons. While Cosimo and his family held the largest shares in these branches, they were in fact self-standing partnerships, with local managers and investors participating in the capital and profits.

To supplement the branches, the Medici also employed local agents and correspondents throughout Europe, providing not only information but also an international structure of credit. The Medici and their correspondents kept accounts open in each others' names, enabling customers to make much greater use of bills of exchange in the early fifteenth century. In 1427, for example, the Medici houses at Florence, Rome and Venice were able to deploy over 62 per cent of their assets in loans and over 20 per cent in accepting bills of exchange from their correspondents (Table 1). This was achieved on a relatively small capital base and, unlike the Bardi and Peruzzi with perhaps ten times the capital commitment, the Medici branches were not dependent upon large royal loans for their earnings. In comparison with their fourteenth-century counterparts, the Medici used their branch network to create a wide 'spread' of business and risk.

The Medici's banking operations were not only ahead of their time in terms of techniques and communications. Their buildings, too, were designed in a grand fashion that reflected the family's political importance, pioneering the notion that banking needed confident, even palatial surroundings. The Medici palace in the Via Larga, Florence, was the centrepiece of this more conspicuous style in the 1440s. Its architect, Michelozzo, was also responsible for the Medici bank in Milan in the 1460s, and his mixing of the needs of business, fortress and palace was the ancestor of bank design down to the twentieth century. Cosimo and his successors, Piero (1416–69) and Lorenzo the Magnificent (1449–92), also emerged as patrons of the arts and letters on a scale which even a modern sponsorship budget could not encompass. Cosimo's extraordinary range of commissions included buildings by Brunelleschi as well as Michelozzo, and he was the principal patron of the sculptor Donatello and the artist Fra Filippo Lippi: Lorenzo also secured a key role in art history as the first patron of Michelangelo and as an important buyer of work by both Verrochio and Botticelli.

In the early fourteenth century the Medici's investments in buildings and in art appear to have been 'off the balance sheet' – that is to say separate from the conduct of banking and trading business. Towards mid-century, however, the heads of the family were prone to mingle the costs of their political and business activities. Lorenzo's enemies even accused him of raiding public funds such as the *Monte Communale* and the *Monte delle Doti*, a dowry fund for girls, to meet business losses. These appropriations were not proved, yet by the 1470s and 1480s it was clear that the bank was at best in difficulty and at worst in terminal decline. The Bruges branch failed soon after its biggest customer, Duke Charles the Bold of Burgundy, was killed in 1477; Lorenzo was also forced to wind up

Lorenzo de Medici, who inherited the premier banking business of Renaissance Italy, emerged as a charismatic figure in politics and in the patronage of the arts in late fifteenth-century Florence. The Medici bank could not sustain the adventures of Lorenzo 'the Magnificent' and after his death in 1492 it lost its position to rival Italian and German banks.

LAVRENTIVS MEDICES PETRI FILIVS.

the London office after defaults by King Edward IV. At Lyons a 'run' on the bank in 1483 added to the firm's distress. The Medici continued to play a leading role in Italian affairs, producing politicians, patrons and the two Medici popes Leo X and Clement VII, but as bankers their ascendancy came to an end with the death of Lorenzo in 1492.

The house of Medici, precocious and colourful as it may have been, was not the only example of bankers' increasing sophistication in the fifteenth century. North of the Alps the meteoric rise of the merchant Jacques Cœur created a major bank-type operation centred on his *hôtel* at Bourges. Cœur was also a trader, an owner of ships and galleys, and a manufacturer whose entangled network of interests was instrumental in the revival of the Mediterranean ports of France in the early fifteenth century. But Cœur became yet another (and by no means the last) of the victims of sovereign lending. In 1451, soon after he

had given a huge loan to Louis XI of France to finance the reconquest of Normandy from the English, Cœur was arrested and his fortune confiscated.

In contrast to the entrepreneurial, single-handed banking ambitions of Jacques Cœur, the Fugger family of Augsburg created a more durable financial dynasty. Originally wool merchants, the Fuggers turned their interests in the fifteenth century to mining and finance. Precious metals and banking were essential allies in their success, since their gold, silver and copper mines in Hungary and Austria emerged as suppliers to coin mints throughout Europe. Having won the monopoly of silver production from the Schwaz mines in Tyrol in 1488, the Fuggers then enjoyed the fruits of a boom in mining for precious metals.

Between the late fifteenth and the mid-sixteenth century this primacy turned the house of Fugger into the most influential and celebrated source of finance on the con-

The *hôtel* headquarters of the financier Jacques Cœur at Bourges. The building was begun in 1443, at the height of Cœur's power as a royal agent, but was not complete at his downfall in 1451. The square holes in the turret attics were for carrier-pigeons, part of Cœur's much-vaunted network of communications.

Jacob Fugger 'the Rich' (1459–1525). The Fugger family of Augsburg created perhaps the most powerful banking dynasty of the Reformation age. Jacob's financial support was essential to the expansion of the Hapsburg empire under Charles V.

The settlement of year-end accounts by a Rouen charity in 1466. Methodical adjustment of credit and cash emerged as a vital part of financial techniques in fourteenth and fifteenth century Europe.

tinent. Jacob Fugger the Rich (1459–1525) became the sole heir to the family's mining and banking operations in 1510, and under his guidance the house became the principal financier to the Habsburg empire in Germany, the Low Countries and Spain. The apex of that power was reached in 1519 with the election of the Habsburg Charles V as Holy Roman Emperor; loans from the Fuggers were deployed on a massive scale to encourage the electors to vote for Charles and against the rival claims of Francis I of France. The success of this enterprise won the Fuggers the role of court bankers throughout the Habsburg empire in the second quarter of the sixteenth century.

The Medici, the Fuggers, and rival houses such as the Pazzi of Florence and the Chigi were the most spectacular banking ventures of the fifteenth and early sixteenth centuries. Although in each case their ascendancy was based upon earlier success as bankers in the world of private enterprise, this prominence was achieved largely through their involvement with the finances of princes and popes. Yet there existed also in fifteenth-century Italy banks which catered for less conspicuous customers – new and unusual financial institutions known as the *monti di pietà*. The function of these banks was to lend small amounts of money at minimal interest to relieve suffering and distress amongst the poor. Loans were for very modest sums, on the security of pledges or pawns. Most of the funds were compiled from charitable donations, although in some cases the *monti* paid interest on deposits and made loans to the wealthy. The earliest *monte di pietà* opened in 1462 in Perugia – a city with a strong tradition of money-dealing and bank-type operations – and provided a model for nearly ninety *monti* throughout Italy fifty years later.

Amongst these establishments was the Monte Pio at Siena. The original unit was a small *monte di pietà* with a capital of only 8,000 florins drawn from the city's funds. There was a maximum of 8 florins for any one loan. After its closure in 1511 a new

Monte Pio was formed in 1569, and in 1625 control passed to the newly-created Monte dei Paschi di Siena, a much larger enterprise with facilities for lending without security and for making grants towards public works projects. Originally described as a *monte non vacabile* – a banking institution which was not to be given up – its capital was guaranteed by the Medici rulers of Siena. Fittingly the *non vacabile* Monte dei Paschi di Siena has outlived its guarantors by more than 250 years.

In the long-term development of banking, the *monti di pietà* and their variants elsewhere (the *huis van leening* which opened in Amsterdam in 1614, for example) made real progress in filtering credit through to the poor and to the artisans and small traders of urban Europe. Nevertheless, the technical advance of banking remained in the hands of those private firms which could survive in international trade and finance. By the sixteenth century, after the long economic stagnation of the late Middle Ages, these firms were operating in very different and very challenging conditions. Population growth and the drain of wealth along the new trade routes

The Palazzo Salembeni, Siena, headquarters of the Monte dei Paschi di Siena. This bank is the successor to the Monte Pio, first opened in the Salembeni in 1472. The monument of the economist Sallustio Bandini is by Tito Sarrochi (1824–1900).

Exchange was a vital ingredient of banking development in Renaissance Italy. This detail of a fresco by Niccolo di Pietro Gerini (at the chapel of San Francisco, Prato, 1395) depicts a money-changer's *banco* or counter.

to the Middle East and Far East increased the demand for coinage and bullion, and despite the huge intake of gold and silver from the Americas (an average of over 110 tons of silver reached Spain each year between 1500 and 1650), this ferment of demand created scarcities of coin throughout the sixteenth century. Such stress in the international economy created all manner of inflationary pressures and trade imbalances and, in the development of banking, these challenges also forced a massive expansion in credit. If coins and bullion were in short supply, then alternative 'bank' currencies could fill the gap. The range of credit techniques was not much changed since the fourteenth century, but bills of exchange and other forms of credit payment were much more widely accepted and traded in the sixteenth century.

Western Europe's international fairs, which had been so important to financial development in the thirteenth century, continued to flourish and were vital to this expansion of credit three centuries later. In the early part of the sixteenth century the Lyons fairs were especially prominent in the settlement of trade payments; there were as many as 169 banking businesses in the city, of which 143 were Italian. These firms used Lyons as their base for the finance of the silk and spice trades, and the close links between the fairs at Lyons and Medina del Campo in Spain were also essential to the inflow of silver in the first half of the century. As many as 2,000 merchants were attending the fairs at Medina in the mid-sixteenth century, and were in residence for at least one quarter of each year.

Nevertheless, the informal market was giving way to a more formal and institutional approach. Cities such as Antwerp (1531), London (1571) and Seville (1583) established their own Bourse or Exchange to act as permanent markets for traders and brokers. Meanwhile the Italians altered both the location and the scope of the traditional fairs. In 1575 the major Genoese firms (whose government was now in alliance with Charles V) pulled out of Lyons

and established their own fair at Besançon, in Hapsburg territory.

There was technical as well as political significance in the Genoese firms' evacuation to Besançon. The Italians were now specialists in foreign exchange, bankers rather than merchants. In 1550, for example, one French commentator found it extraordinary that the Italians would travel to the fairs empty-handed, and without . . .

This allegory by Jost Amman gives a dramatic view of the German business scene in the late sixteenth century. Money-changing and ledger-keeping are well to the fore, and the allegory emphasizes the importance of Discretion, Integrity, and Knowledge of languages in the financial world.

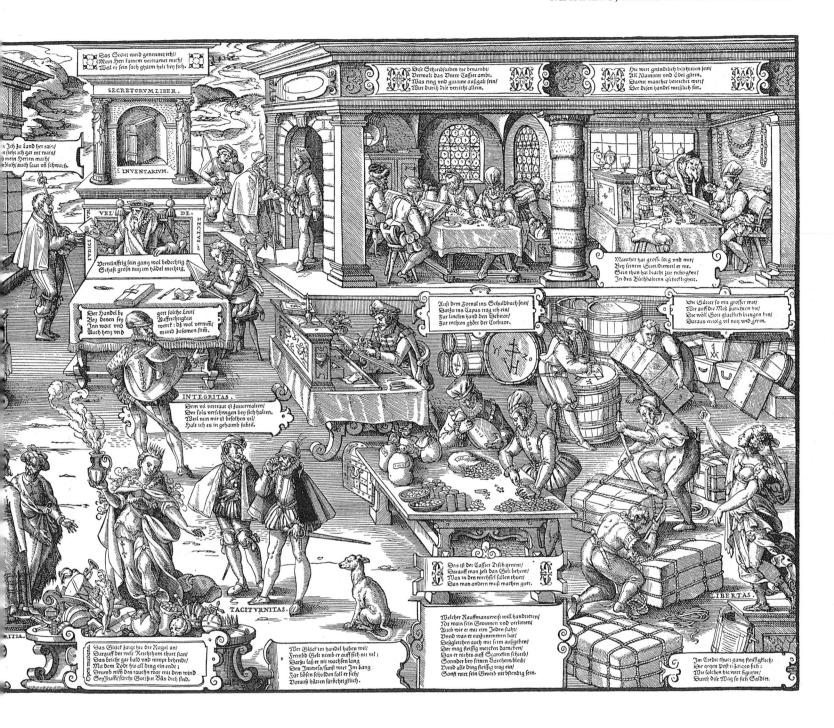

… anything besides their persons, with a little credit, a pen, ink and paper, and skill in handling, turning and diverting the exchanges from one country to another, according to the information they have of the places where money is dearest.

From the middle of the century the Genoese were moving into a 'golden age' of banking and finance. In 1579 they transplanted their four-times-yearly fairs from Besançon, via Poligny and Chambéry to their own Genoan city of Piacenza. Throughout these wanderings the markets kept their title of 'Besançon fairs'. Between fifty and sixty banking firms, *banchieri di conto*, controlled dealings at the fairs with perhaps twice as many trading firms in attendance to settle their international tran-

The 'Joseph Window' of Chartres Cathedral was installed in about 1210. This section, depicting the counters or money-changers, was probably based upon the exchange shops on the south side of the cathedral, in the area now known as the Rue des Changes.

Il Negotiante of 1638, by Domenico Peri of Genoa, offered a comprehensive view of the commercial practices of the 'Besançon fairs' which had played a key role in international banking in the sixteenth and early seventeenth centuries. This title page is taken from the 1682 edition published in Venice.

the royal borrowers, and in the first part of the century its banking needs continued to be supplied by the Fuggers and their associates the Welser and Hochstätter banks of Augsburg. By mid-century, however, Charles V and his heir Philip II of Spain were faced with political and religious challenges throughout Europe. The drain on imperial resources led, in 1557, to Philip's declaration of bankruptcy, in the aftermath of which the Fuggers and their banking allies could no longer sustain their lending. In their place Genoese bankers such as the Grimaldi and Gentile provided new loans to Philip – usually with 'penalty' interest clauses, and complex conditions for payments and bullion shipments between Spain and the Genoese agents in Italy and Flanders.

The management of payments to Flanders was especially important to Philip II, as the war in the Low Countries demanded vast sums for army pay and provisions. Spain, France and England were all embroiled in the war after 1572 and in each case their war finances needed the intermediation of the Italian and German bankers.

sactions. Each representative would bring to Piacenza the *scartafaccio* or bill book of his firm and would settle outstanding debts or payments before the end of each fair. These clearing operations also meant that the Besançon fairs saw relatively few deals in cash or bullion while millions of *scudi* were either paid by credit or rolled forward to the next fair.

The liberation of credit payments, particularly through the Genoese firms, had a double significance. Firstly, the financial and business community began to enjoy the benefits of lower interest rates as the expanding opportunities for 'clearing' payments, combined with less hostile attitudes to interest charges after the Reformation, drove down the price of borrowing in the later sixteenth century. Secondly, the pre-eminence of the Genoese bankers in the later sixteenth century altered the balance of sovereign debt in Europe. The Habsburg empire of Charles V was by far the largest of

Sir Thomas Gresham, whose business was based at *The Grasshopper* in Lombard Street, London, acted as financial agent to the government of Queen Elizabeth I. Gresham was a key figure in the reform of the English coinage and was the instigator of the Royal Exchange in 1566. From a portrait of 1565, artist unknown.

In the Spanish case, the Genoese banks were transmitting an annual average of 5.5 million florins to the Netherlands between 1561 and 1610. Three times that amount was transmitted in the pre-Armada year of 1587, mostly by bill of exchange. Whenever the Genoese bankers' domination was challenged, their payments system proved remarkably effective and durable. In 1575, for example, Philip struck back at his bankers by annulling all loan agreements since 1560, believing over-optimistically that the Fuggers and Spanish merchant bankers such as the Ruiz and Espinosa could take the Italians' place. The Genoese bankers responded by blocking payments of gold and bills of exchange to Flanders. So successful was this manœuvre that the unpaid Spanish army in Flanders mutinied and sacked Antwerp in 1576. Philip had little choice but to negotiate with the Italians and reinstall them as his bankers in 1577.

Throughout the sixteenth century bankers such as the Fuggers and the Genoese played an essentially *entrepreneurial* role in public finance. Their banking services relied upon their flexibility as private firms, their familiarity with the international fairs, and the relative efficiency of their payments between European centres of trade. But perhaps the most striking feature of this entrepreneurial style of public lending was the fragility of sources of funds. Ironically, at a time when the techniques of payment were more widely used, the numbers of banking units in Europe were still falling. In Florence, where there had been eighty firms in banking before the Black Death, only eight banks remained at the beginning of the sixteenth century. Similarly, in 1585 it was estimated that ninety-six of the one hundred and three private banks founded in Venice to date had closed or failed. Bank failures continued into the second half of the sixteenth century, narrowing the sources of credit into the hands of the larger firms.

Mismanagement, an often hostile cultural environment, and the effects of severe inflation all increased the vulnerability of private banking firms. For the largest firms – those who had made the transition from international banking to public finance – the greatest danger was still the volatile nature of European politics. The Genoese bankers at the court of Spain were masters in terms of capital resources and techniques, yet in 1575 they had faced failure both in Spain and in their own city. After their return as Philip II's bankers they were severely tested by further state bankruptcies in 1596 and 1607. It was political opposition which would eventually drive them from the seat of power in Spain in 1627.

This vulnerability of bankers to sovereign debts had been a constant theme of the early development of banking since the fourteenth century. The Florentine dynasties, the Fuggers and the Genoese bankers all suffered eventually from their status as private or family businesses. At a time when the demands of state finance were increasing at a tremendous rate, the numbers and resources of private bankers could not keep pace indefinitely. Stability and larger resources could only come from a more permanent, *institutional* approach to public finance. It was this clarification of public and private finance that dominated the next phases of banking development.

CHAPTER TWO

THE STRUGGLE FOR STABILITY

Banking in the 17th and 18th centuries

Years, decades and even centuries have passed between the first appearance of a technical development and its adoption on a large, international scale. In banking history significant breakthroughs were made in the medieval and early modern period, and in some cases the new techniques and institutions were widely reported throughout Europe. But their adoption on a more permanent footing and on a larger scale was none the less delayed until the seventeenth and eighteenth centuries, an era which gave birth to some of the modern world's leading financial institutions.

Political and economic conditions in the seventeenth century were not the most promising setting for durable progress in banking. After a brief truce in the fighting in the Low Countries in the second decade of the century, the much larger conflict of the Thirty Years War entangled most of Europe between 1618 and 1648. The price in terms of manpower and war finance fell heavily on the German territories of the Habsburg empire but this ruination was part of much wider economic distress in the mid-seventeenth century. By the end of the century the military ambitions of Louis XIV brought further economic and monetary turmoil, and it was not until the 1720s that the financial community was permitted a more stable political platform.

The Europe-wide appetite for war payments in the seventeenth century ensured that public finance remained the most prominent theme of banking development;

there was indeed a pressing need for institutions which were large enough to manage such expenditure but secure and impersonal enough to escape the fate of the private bankers of the previous century. The city-states of Europe were well ahead of the major nation-states in developing institutional banking units. In most cases these solutions were intended to bring order to public debt rather than provide war finance, but they were to be influential examples for the nation-state banks of the seventeenth and eighteenth centuries.

In the Italian city-states, the tradition of converting public debts into bank-type operations reached back to the thirteenth century (see p. 13). From the mid-sixteenth century, however, the Italians were developing banks in which the State was either a full partner or the guarantor of its funds. For instance, the Bank of Palermo, founded in 1551, was protected by the guarantee of the city's senate; its main functions were the collection of taxes and the management of the State's payments and coinage. A similar enterprise, the Tavola della Citta di Messina, was launched in Sicily in 1587. Meanwhile the Casa di San Giorgio at Genoa, which had continued as a formal association of the State's creditors since the fifteenth century, resumed its operations as a deposit bank in the 1580s, and it was to continue in that role until its assets were confiscated by the French in 1800.

This transition to institutional finance was especially successful (if somewhat prolonged) at Venice, where the Banco della Piazza di Rialto was authorized by a decree of the Senate in 1584 and opened in 1587. Guaranteed by the State, the bank took deposits, accepted bills of exchange and made credit transfers between accounts. The Rialto Bank none the less did not have the whole-hearted support of the Senate, which in the early seventeenth century restricted its activities on the grounds that it was making excessive profits on state-guaranteed bonds. Intervention was taken even further in 1619, when the Senate founded the Banco del Giro with the task of managing the public debt and operating accounts for the State's creditors so that;

> . . . in the said same bank they should be given prompt and immediate satisfaction of their credits from divers markets, bills of exchange and other dues . . . in order thus to escape the delays and obstacles which . . . are very frequently the case.

The Banco del Giro's main advantage in taking on this role was the State's guarantee of the interest-bearing bonds issued by the bank to the State's creditors. These *partite* were fully transferable and tradable, and they circulated at the handsome premium of 20 per cent. When the *partite* depreciated rapidly during an economic and military crisis in the early 1630s, the Senate intervened by buying them back and restoring their value. This type of confidence-boosting commitment, in complete contrast to the state defaults of the previous century, led to the transfer of many accounts to the Banco del Giro in the middle decades of the century. Thereafter the bank consolidated its position as the agent for the State's creditors, and from 1666 onwards it also opened accounts for private and business customers depositing cash with the bank. In this role it survived until the French invasion of Italy in 1797.

Successful and durable as these Italian experiments were, they were produced by city-states which were no longer at the centre of economic and financial power.

Their ancient textile industries were increasingly pushed aside by English and Dutch imports, while the great fairs at Piacenza were displaced by the new bourses in Antwerp, Amsterdam, Seville and London. In such conditions the Italian city-states could not sustain their leadership in finance and banking: for all the sophistication of their techniques and institutions, they were not coping with the demands of an expanding nation-state and a growing economy. In the seventeenth century these demands were increasingly centred on northern Europe – on London, Paris, the Baltic ports and, above all, Amsterdam.

Amsterdam's economic ascendancy was sudden and almost unchallenged. Antwerp's pre-eminence had come to an end when the city was captured by the Spanish in 1585. Amsterdam then emerged from relative obscurity to become the leading international market for shipping, commodities and capital; its maritime and inland trade spread its influence throughout Europe and into the new commercial outposts of Asia, Africa and the Americas. This extraordinary career was not built on weak foundations. Almost from the start of its ascendancy, Amsterdam and its citizens favoured an institutional and rule-based approach to business. The Amsterdam Chamber of Assurance, for example, was established in 1598; the joint-stock United East India Company was promoted in 1602; the new bourse opened in 1608; and a grain exchange was commissioned in 1616. In this style the city's rise to financial pre-eminence was strikingly speedy.

Central to this institutional structure was the Amsterdam Wisselbank or Exchange Bank. The promotion of the Wisselbank was approved by the city council in 1606 and it was opened in 1609. Influenced by the model of the Rialto public bank in Venice, the Wisselbank was authorized to receive deposits and bills of exchange and to transfer payments between its customers' accounts; lending was restricted to the City of Amsterdam itself, the Province of Holland, and the United East India Company. This restriction was eventually relaxed in 1683, when the Wisselbank was permitted to advance funds to private customers on the security of gold and silver deposits.

The power and ubiquity of the Wisselbank were based solidly on its home market of public institutions and the merchants of Amsterdam. Indeed, it was a requirement that all bills valued at over 600 florins should be paid through the bank, in effect forcing all the major houses to open accounts there. As a result the number of accounts multiplied from 730 in 1609 to about 2,000 in the 1660s and 2,700 by the end of the seventeenth century. Total deposits, which were guaranteed by the city, averaged about 7 million florins between 1640 and 1685 – equivalent to 8 per cent of the entire wealth of the city – and doubled to over 16 million florins by 1700 (see Table 2). Although the Wisselbank did not play such an overt role in public finance as the Banco del Giro at Venice, direct lending to the City of Amsterdam accounted for as much as one fifth of the bank's assets. The bank's official responsibility for coinage and exchange also contributed to its profitability and stability. Not least, the Wisselbank's reputation for both security and convenience attracted business from foreign governments as well as international traders. Sir William Temple, in his *Observations upon the United Provinces* of 1673, described how:

> Foreigners lodge here what part of their Money they could transport, and knew no way of securing at home. Nor did those People only lodge Moneys here, who came over into the Country; but many more who never left their own; Though they provided for a retreat, or against a Storm, and thought no place so secure as this, nor from whence they might so easily draw their Money into any parts of the World.

Amongst those thought to have 'provided for a retreat' in this way were members of the English Commonwealth Parliament and the Danish court, the Prince Palatine and the Republic of Venice. The Wisselbank was also used by the Spanish crown to pay subsidies to Sweden in the 1660s. To this extent the Wisselbank was not only a public bank for Amsterdam and its citizens but also a secure haven for other European governments and political interests. Its success continued well into the eighteenth century, even after Amsterdam's ascendancy was coming to an end, and it survived until 1820.

The Wisselbank's role as a deposit-taking and exchange bank was soon reproduced in many of the other leading city-states of northern Europe. Similar banks were founded at Middelburg in the United Provinces in 1616, Hamburg (1619), Nuremberg (1621), Delft (1621) and Rotterdam (1635). Like the Wisselbank, the Hamburg version also acted as a magnet for foreign accounts, even serving as a go-between bank when the United Provinces were at war with England in the third quarter of the century.

The Wisselbank and its imitators were inextricably linked to the financial and monetary regimes of their own city-states. Yet they did not attempt, and they were not required, to carry the full weight of sovereign debt in the same way that the Fuggers and the Genoese bankers had in the sixteenth century. This was clearly an area where institutional solutions might offer greater financial continuity to the nation-states of Europe and, perhaps, greater security to promoters and investors in banking. When the expenditure of the major powers again accelerated rapidly in the middle of the seventeenth century, the management of state debt emerged as a guiding theme of banking development.

The notion of an official 'state bank' was already in circulation at the end of the sixteenth century. In 1576, in answer to Spain's serious debt problems and as a counter to the supremacy of the Genoese bankers, the Flemish merchant Peter van Oudegherste had outlined a plan for a

Founded in 1619, the Banco del Giro of Venice, Italy, was initially a State bank and then (from 1666) a deposit bank. Gabriel Bella's painting of the bank on the Rialto dates from the mid-eighteenth century.

The courtyard of the Amsterdam Bourse in 1668, by Job Berckheyde. This commercial exchange, together with the city's Wisselbank and chamber of assurance, made Amsterdam the most integrated and highly sophisticated financial market of the seventeenth century.

Spanish state bank. The same idea was canvassed by Spanish bankers in 1583. A proposal to form a 'Banque de France' was presented to Henri IV of France as early as 1608. The first plan to reach fruition, however, was the foundation of the Riksbank, or Bank of Sweden, in 1668. The Riksbank's activities were modelled on the deposit and exchange role of the Wisselbank, with the important difference that its principal customer was an ambitious and expanding nation-state rather than a city corporation. Sweden was also the setting for an important experiment in bank currency. Johan Palmstruch, founder of the Bank of Stockholm in 1656, devised a paper currency to take the place of copper coins. Printed notes, *Kreditivsedlar*, were first circulated in 1661. They were effectively the earliest banknotes to appear on the European scene – predated only by the paper currency circulating during the Chinese Ming dynasty (1368–1694) which in turn was claimed to have originated in seventh century China. The issue of Palmstruch's notes subsequently ran out of control and the experiment was suspended in 1664.

It was not until the foundation of the Bank of England in 1694 that the potential scope of a state bank became obvious. This enterprise, like so many of its forerunners in the city-states and nation-states of Europe, owed its birth and early upbringing to a long-running accumulation of government debt.

Throughout the seventeenth century, including the period of the Civil War and Commonwealth, the English government was in almost continual debt. Traditionally the deficit was financed by the unedifying blend of selling land, confiscation, and the dishonouring of debts. The government also borrowed heavily from City of London merchants. The goldsmiths were an especially significant source of funds, and although this group had been accepting deposits of cash as well as valuables since the early years of the century, the turmoil of the Civil War made their safe-custody and payments services increasingly popular

amongst the merchants of London. (These operations were subsequently a factor in the growth of private banking in England (see p. 45).) During the Commonwealth, Edward Backwell, Robert Vyner, Isaac Meynell and other goldsmiths were active in discounting and issuing bills of exchange (including official payments). Backwell, described by Samuel Pepys as 'the great money man' and often claimed to be 'the father of English banking', also acted as a contractor to the government by taking deposits from other goldsmiths and lending on to the Treasury. Then, after the Res-

Edward Backwell, the grandest of the goldsmith-bankers of London in the later seventeenth century. Backwell acted as the government's financial agent – including the management of the sale of Dunkirk to the French in 1662. Charles II's suspension of repayments forced him out of business in the 1670s.

toration, the goldsmith-bankers were tied more closely to financial policy, and their co-operation was an important factor in the creation of a new form of English public debt in the 1660s. The introduction of 'orders in payment' in 1665 made it possible for government departments to issue assignable 'promises to pay' to its creditors. The London goldsmiths accepted the orders on a large scale, swelling their asset-holdings in the late 1660s.

Sovereign debt remained a high-risk operation for these private entrepreneurs, however, and Backwell and the other leading goldsmith-bankers were undone by a panic in the City in 1671. The government, unable to honour over £2 million worth of orders, placed its 'Stop of the Exchequer' on any orders not repayable from certain future revenue. This suspension of payments froze £1.3 million owing to the goldsmiths, many of whom were ruined, and Backwell himself could only struggle on in a small way for another ten years.

The Crown's heavy-handed response in

1671 in effect ended the goldsmiths' role in the fragile recovery of English public finance. Yet the State's indebtedness continued to deepen, especially when the new government of William III and Mary embarked on war with France in 1689. A more permanent, institutional form of borrowing was badly needed if public confidence in the government's debt was to be restored. The breakthrough, when it came, was by an unusual route. William Paterson, a Scots entrepreneur, was one of a group of 'projectors' who in the 1680s and 1690s were bombarding English investors with schemes for new joint-stock enterprises, and an ambitious proposal of his in 1694 won the support of Charles Montagu, the Chancellor of the Exchequer. In return for a loan to the government of £1.2 million at 8 per cent, the subscribers were allowed to form a corporation under the title of 'The Governor and Company of the Bank of England', with a minimum life of twelve years. The Bank would have joint-stock status, with ownership in the hands of private

The ledgers of Edward Backwell, the London goldsmith-banker, are amongst the oldest and most remarkable sets of business archives. This example is open at a page analysing the account of Samuel Pepys, the diarist and man of affairs.

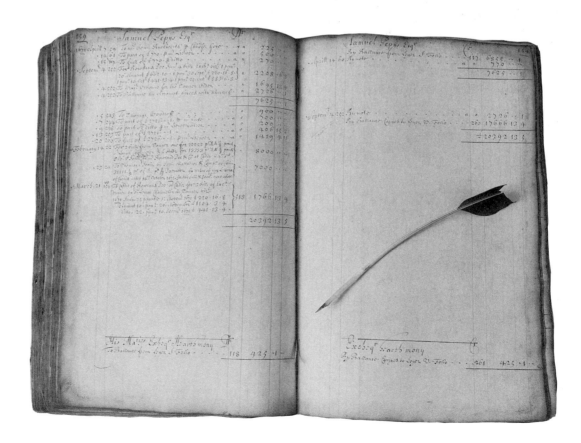

The Court Room of the Bank of England, London, designed by Sir Robert Taylor in 1760s. Later relocated from the ground floor to the first floor, the room remains the venue for meetings of directors of the Bank.

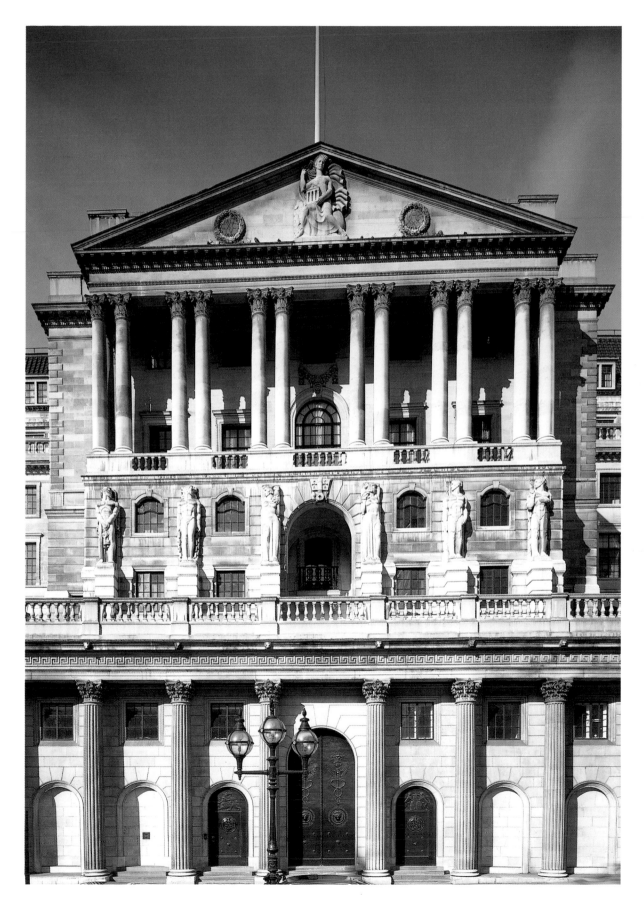

The Threadneedle Street entrance and façade of the Bank of England, London. The exterior of the modern Bank was entirely remodelled by Sir Herbert Baker in the 1920s and the 1930s, leaving only the outer ground floor walls designed by Sir John Soane in 1788.

shareholders. The original loan, launched in June 1694, was fully subscribed within twelve days and the 1,272 original subscribers were granted their charter in July. The initial loan and additional borrowings through the Bank enabled the Treasury to sustain the finance of the French war until the Treaty of Rijswick in 1697.

The new Bank of England was not simply a loan agency for the government. It was also prepared to redeem Exchequer orders in payment and it agreed that its own 'sealed bills' or promissory notes could be issued by the Treasury to the government's creditors. It handled the payment of the army in Flanders, entered the foreign exchange and bullion market, opened accounts for private customers (including the goldsmith-bankers of London), and accepted and paid the bills of exchange of its customers. The issue of banknotes, though not mentioned in the original legislation, almost immediately became a distinctive feature of the new company.

Within five years of its foundation, the Bank's notes in circulation were worth over £1.3 million and by 1720 the total approached £2.5 million. The size and flexibility of the note-issue was unique for a single banking institution.

The breadth of the Bank of England's operations owed much to the efficiency of its management. From the outset the Governor and the Court of twenty-five Directors were merchants with the highest level of reputation and experience. Sir John Houblon, for example, who was the first Governor, came from a merchant family specializing in trade with France and the Mediterranean, and like seven of the other founding directors he was from a Huguenot background. Their success in the Bank's first years won them the renewal of the corporation's charter and, in 1708, the privilege of being the only banking unit permitted to have more than six partners. These rewards gave to the Bank an unchallenged position at the centre of English

Threadneedle Street, London, in about 1730, with the Bank of England at the centre and the Lottery Office at the right of the picture.

finance – a supremacy which had the backing of government and of legislation. In return the English government leaned heavily on the Bank in the early decades of the eighteenth century. Between 1710 and 1714 the bank was commissioned to receive the proceeds of government lotteries, and in 1717 it was given the management of the 'consolidated' fund of long-term government debt. After the speculative mania of the South Sea Bubble, leading to the collapse in stock of the government-sponsored South Sea Company in 1720, it also played an essential 'rescue' role by buying £4.2 million of the collapsed South Sea stock. In this guise the Bank was a key factor in the stabilization of public borrowing in the remainder of the eighteenth century.

The formation of the Bank of Sweden and, more especially, the foundation of the Bank of England had shown that institutional banks could survive the heavy demands of leading nation-states. Serious efforts were made to follow their example

elsewhere in Europe. In France, at Louis XIV's death in 1715, the State's indebtedness had reached nearly 3,000 million *livres*, dwarfing its annual revenues of only 80 million *livres*. A systematic attempt to rein in the debt was made by John Law, a Scottish exile advising the French regency. Law keenly favoured institutional solutions – the Ferme Générale to collect indirect taxes, the old-established Compagnie des Indes, reorganized as a state monopoly for overseas trade, and the Banque Générale. The Banque, which was founded as a private company in 1716, became a state monopoly under the title of the Banque Royale two years later.

For the moment it appeared that Law had succeeded in building a unified financial structure. However, one serious weakness remained. The Banque had been issuing very large numbers of banknotes in an effort to revive the French economy. Nearly a billion *livres* were issued in notes in 1719 and by October 1720 2.7 billion *livres* in

A room in the Bank of England in about 1695, from one of the earliest illustrations of the new institution. At that time the Bank was housed at Grocer's Hall, Poultry, where it continued until the move to Threadneedle Street in 1734.

notes issued by the Banque were in circulation. This massive expansion of credit contributed to a sudden inflation and a rush by investors to convert their holdings of government debt into shares in the Compagnie des Indes. Paris was by now sharing the speculative mania which engulfed London, Amsterdam and even Switzerland. In the spring of 1720 investors throughout Europe were pouring funds into the English South Sea Company but, when the 'Bubble' burst in August, French as well as English stock prices were flattened. Holdings in the Compagnie des Indes became practically worthless and on 1 November the notes of the Banque ceased to be legal tender. Law was forced out of the country (he died in poverty in Venice in 1729) and his Compagnie and Banque were both dis-

solved. Investments and savings throughout France vanished as the government repudiated or converted most of the outstanding debts, leaving behind an inheritance of hostility and suspicion towards the centralization of banking and finance. Private banking firms survived in this climate but the notion of institutional banking withered. It was not until the formation of the Banque de France in 1800 that Law's ambitions for a unified financial system were to be fulfilled (see p. 56).

Elsewhere on the international financial scene, the development of state banking institutions was patchy. In Germany Frederick the Great of Prussia authorized a note-issuing bank, the Königliche Giro- und Lehnbanco, in 1765 but its growth was restricted by Frederick's reluctance to deposit

A perspective view of the Bank of England, designed by George Sampson and completed in 1734. This view shows the Threadneedle Street entrance in the foreground and the Pay Hall in the centre.

Bowler Miller, Chief Clerk of the 3% Consol's Office at the Bank of England, from an engraving published by Vickery in 1790. In the eighteenth and nineteenth centuries careers in banking could be very long indeed. Miller, for example, was employed by the Bank of England for half a century.

A Victorian view of seventeenth-century banking. In *The Banker's Private Room* by John Callcot Horsley (1817–1903), a loan is being negotiated – without too much regard for confidentiality.

his own treasury funds with the bank. Consequently the note-issue remained small and was eventually suspended in 1806. In contrast, the Anspach-Bayreuth Bank (established in 1780, the forerunner of the Bayerische Vereinsbank) acted as a royal treasury as well as a credit institution. It survived the complex transfer of Anspach-Bayreuth from Prussian to Bavarian sovereignty in 1805 to become one of the leading banking operations in southern Germany.

Spanish efforts to create a national bank were less successful. The Bank of St Charles was established in 1782, partly in support of Spain's role in the American War of Independence. Promoted by the French entrepreneur François Cabarrus, this experiment failed in 1808 when the bank could not redeem the Spanish crown's large floating debt.

In America itself, the position was complicated both by the inborn distrust of centralization and the lack of a standard currency. Under the Constitution of 1789, however, the management of the currency was finally placed in the hands of the United States Treasury, while the foundation of the Bank of the United States two years later provided for the issue of dollar notes, the discount of bills and the management of government debts. Although the Bank's charter was not renewed in 1811 (see p. 57), its brief career set a precedent for a national banking institution over and above the individual States of the union.

The institutional approach to banking was not always in support of public debt. An important exception to the general pattern was the Scottish banking tradition. In 1695, immediately after the foundation of the Bank of England, the Edinburgh-based Bank of Scotland was promoted as a joint-stock corporation. It was a *national* bank in the sense that its proprietors were required to be naturalized Scots, but it differed from other public banks by being forbidden to lend to the State. It was designed mainly for Scottish business and private customers, and this principle was maintained after the Anglo-Scottish Act of Union in 1707. A rival group of investors launched a similar joint-stock company, the Royal Bank of Scotland, in 1727. Like the Bank of Scotland, the Royal Bank issued its own notes but its system of 'cash credits' (devised in 1728) was a vital step in the development of the modern bank overdraft. In the absence of the monopoly legislation which ruled in England, a further joint-stock concern began banking in 1746. This company, the British Linen Company of Edinburgh, was based upon an earlier trading and industrial enterprise, but its entry into banking in 1746 added competition as well as stability to the Scottish banking scene.

Even before the foundation of the Bank

A circular note issued by the Paris branch of Sir Robert Herries and Co., London, in the 1770s. These notes were provided for travellers in Europe, foreshadowing the introduction of travellers cheques in the later nineteenth century.

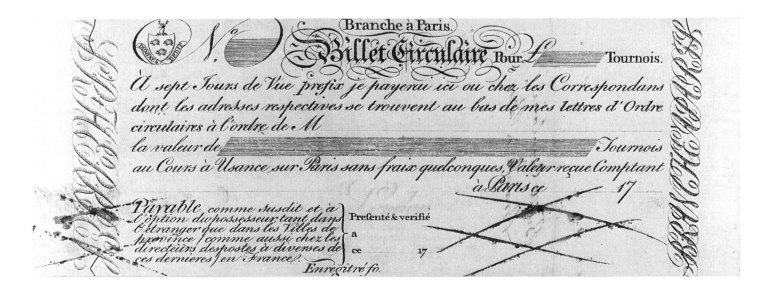

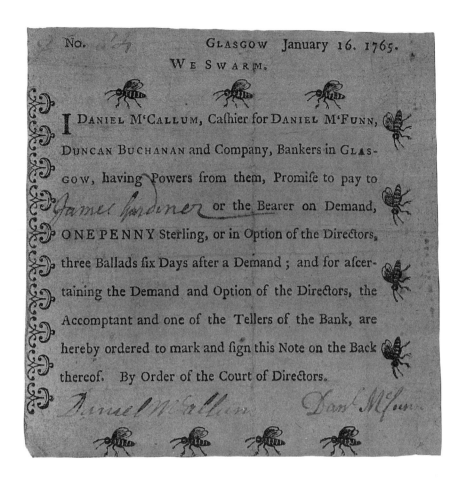

No. GLASGOW January 16. 1765.

WE SWARM.

I DANIEL M'CALLUM, Cashier for DANIEL M'FUNN, DUNCAN BUCHANAN and Company, Bankers in GLAS-GOW, having Powers from them, Promise to pay to *James Gardiner* or the Bearer on Demand, ONE PENNY Sterling, or in Option of the Directors, three Ballads six Days after a Demand; and for ascer-taining the Demand and Option of the Directors, the Accomptant and one of the Tellers of the Bank, are hereby ordered to mark and sign this Note on the Back thereof. By Order of the Court of Directors.

A 'skit' note published in Glasgow in 1765. Bank notes were frequently the target for lampoons as well as the more sinister work of forgery.

of England in 1694 (and the consequent creation of a more secure financial background for businesses and private individuals), there was a recognizable tradition of private banking in England. The goldsmith-bankers of London had provided safe custody and accepted customers' deposits since the early seventeenth century. Customers could use 'drawn notes' to authorize their goldsmith-bankers to make payments from their accounts to third parties. The goldsmiths' own notes, carrying the now familiar terminology of 'I promise to pay', emerged as a form of banking currency in the London market. It was mainly the smaller firms, those not embroiled in government finance, who survived the 1670s crisis (see p. 37), and the unknown author of *The Mystery of the New Fashioned Goldsmiths* (1676) describes them providing a variety of cashiering and exchange services. Many of the longest-surviving London banks descended from this group –

notably Hoare's Bank (founded at the 'Golden Bottle' in Cheapside in 1673), Coutts (originally established by John Campbell in 1692), and Child and Co (who began banking in 1673 and are now part of the Royal Bank of Scotland). Over the next century these firms and their contemporaries gradually dropped their goldsmith associations and became banking specialists. By 1770 there were no less than fifty private banks in London and at the end of the century the total had increased to seventy. Some, like Martins (founded in 1712) and Glyns (1753), were based primarily in the City of London money market, where they could specialize in discounting and exchange. Others, like Coutts, Childs, and Drummonds (founded in 1717) installed themselves in the West End to serve the aristocracy and the politicians and office-holders of Westminster.

The goldsmiths had a significant and sometimes glamorous role in the history of private banking. Equally if not more important, however, was the 'scrivener' tradition in English banking. Since the sixteenth century scriveners had supplied a range of law services from handwriting and searches of title to mortgage-broking and conveyancing. In the Elizabethan period they were also receiving cash-deposits from provincial merchants, and by the seventeenth century these 'money-scriveners' were using their expertise in property to handle large and complex financial transactions. By the third quarter of the century they had become a powerful influence on banking development.

The firm of Clayton and Morris, scriveners of Old Jewry, was especially prominent between its formation in 1658 and the 1690s. The business was substantial. By the end of the firm's three-year account in 1677, for instance, deposits exceeded £1.8 million. This was probably a larger scale of operation than the business of the largest goldsmith-bankers who had been so damaged by the Stop of the Exchequer in 1671. There is also evidence that it was the scrivener-bankers rather than the goldsmiths

A one guinea note issued by the Royal Bank of Scotland, Edinburgh, in 1777, from the first series of British notes to be printed in three colours. Low-denomination notes were – and remain – a distinctive feature of the Scottish banking system.

West Country banking in England: Stuckey's Bank was established in Langport, Somerset, in 1772 and during the nineteenth century it emerged as one of the largest and strongest of the English country banks. This watercolour by Arthur Parkman shows the Castle Bank (otherwise known as the Dutch House) which served as Stuckey's office in Bristol from 1826 to 1854. Stuckey's Bank was acquired in 1909 by Parr's Bank, a constituent part of National Westminster Bank.

who were in the van of banking techniques in seventeenth-century England. The earliest surviving cheque, dated 16 February 1659 (p. 49), was drawn on an account with 'Mr Morris & Mr Clayton'. Distantly descended from early Italian examples of negotiable payments (see p. 16), this form of cheque was a direct development of written authorizations used in the English scrivener banks earlier in the 1650s. By the 1660s Clayton and Morris were also issuing 'promise to pay' banknotes in the same style as those of the London goldsmiths.

The firm of Clayton and Morris was not a permanent feature of the banking scene: the business could not long survive the death of Sir Robert Clayton in 1707. Nevertheless, as Frank Melton has recently shown, the scrivener-bankers had developed a network of deposits and mortgages which carried banking techniques and routines outside London. At first provincial customers, mainly landowners and cattle merchants, depended heavily upon their London banks for deposits and loans. Before the middle decades of the eighteenth century they had little choice; for, although Smith and Co of Nottingham (established in 1659) and the Gurneys of Norwich could handle bills of exchange and other payments, they were very early and exceptional cases. Then from the

Portrait of Sir Robert Clayton, the great scrivener-banker, by Lorenzo da Castro, circa 1680. The firm of Clayton and Morris was a pioneer of private deposit banking in England; Clayton was also a director of the Bank of England between 1702 and his death in 1707.

From the 1650s at the latest the customers of English scrivener-bankers used 'drawn notes' (later known as cheques) to pay third parties or to draw cash from their own accounts. This example, drawn on the firm of Clayton and Morris, is the earliest surviving English cheque.

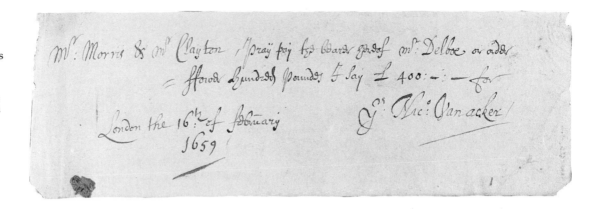

English country banking: the Gurneys, a Quaker family in Norfolk, began banking business in 1775. Two years later they moved to this building at Bank Plain, Norwich, and a series of other Gurney banks were opened throughout East Anglia. The Gurney banks were important constituents of the modern Barclays Bank.

middle of the eighteenth century a new breed of 'country banks' gave England and Wales the beginnings of a local banking system.

Like the scriveners, many country bankers entered the business through another professional or business route. Some were merchants, manufacturers and especially brewers who diversified into banking in order to sharpen up their own methods of payments and receipts. In 1765, for example, the ironmaster Samuel Lloyd and John Taylor, a button manufacturer, established a banking firm in Birmingham (the ancestor of Lloyds Bank). Others, such as tax receivers and the officials of canal companies and turnpikes, moved into banking to deploy the funds entrusted to them – a perfectly legal operation at that time, in which receivers and officials had the advantage of close contact with the London market. In addition to scriveners, law attorneys were also well placed to hold money for clients and eventually to act as lending bankers.

The Pay Hall at the Bank of England, London, designed by George Sampson in 1734. Thomas Rowlandson's drawing (published by Ackermann in 1808) shows a melée of investors in government stocks: the structure in the centre was an elaborate charcoal-burning stove.

'A March to the Bank' by James Gillray, 1787. After the Gordon Riots of 1780, when the Bank of England had come under violent attack, a permanent night duty of regimental guards was mounted at the Bank. Initially the 'Bank Picquet' was greatly resented in Westminster and the City of London but the tradition continued until 1973.

From this mixture of origins the country banks emerged as a distinctive feature of the provincial scene in England and Wales. Numbering no more than a dozen in the early eighteenth century, they proliferated in the second half of the century to a total of 334 by 1797 and over 600 by 1810. Those in rural areas usually limited their operations to receiving deposits and sending their customers' bills to London banks (or agents). Those in the growing industrial territories were more active in lending – either through advances or by discounting bills; they also needed the help of London agents at times of heavy demand. In most cases the country banks issued their own notes as a form of local banking currency, although the industrial areas of Lancashire and the West Riding of Yorkshire relied more upon bills and promissory notes for the settlement of debts.

In Scotland also, the appearance of the first major banking institutions had created a more fruitful climate for provincial banking. In the middle decades of the eighteenth century private banks were formed in Glasgow, Aberdeen, Dundee and Perth, despite the opposition of the joint-stock banks in Edinburgh. A variation on the same theme was the Ayr Bank of 1769, a joint-stock concern which vigorously extended a network of branches in the principal cities of Scotland. Within three years, however, the Ayr Bank's lending was completely out of control and it failed in June 1772. Although in Edinburgh as many as thirteen private bankers failed in the aftermath of this collapse, the Scottish provincial banks survived and flourished, and by 1810 Scotland was served by twenty-five such banks in addition to the three public banks of Edinburgh.

The development of provincial banking in the eighteenth century was not confined to the British Isles. Across the Atlantic, a provincial banking tradition began to emerge after the American War of Independence. The States of the union chartered their own banks while private banking firms issued their own 'scrip money' notes for local circulation. The Bank of North America, although chartered by the United States Congress, was essentially a regional bank when it opened for business in 1782. Yet none of the overseas examples were on the same scale or in the same numbers as the British country banks. Towards the end of the eighteenth century England, Wales and Scotland were still the only cases where deposit banking was a familiar part of the community in small rural centres as well as in major towns and cities.

The banking and financial institutions of seventeenth century Europe had intro-

The 'Grasshopper': Sir Thomas Gresham, financial agent to Queen Elizabeth I, adopted the grasshopper shop sign outside his goldsmith's shop in Lombard Street in the 1560s. The original sign was destroyed in the Great Fire of London in 1666 but this version was used by the Martin banking family from about 1670.

A cartoon account of the Ayr Bank collapse in 1772. The Scottish bankers are caricatured as bewitching investors and draining off English gold to finance 'Charly', the Stuart pretender to the throne. The disconsolate figure at the right of the picture had been devising a 'Scheme for Paying Off the National Debt'.

duced more system and more continuity into the ever-troublesome management of public debt. As the eighteenth century reached its close, however, banking business was facing a different order of need. The revolutionary wars in America and France were again raising the stakes of international conflict; the enlargement of the European empires was stretching the boundaries of the international economy; and the steady spread of industrialization and mechanization was introducing entirely new patterns of demand for financial support. Banking, fast though it had developed in the seventeenth and eighteenth centuries, could only meet these needs by adapting its structure and techniques. To the still small banking industry, the challenge was to serve a market which was larger and wealthier *per capita*, more industrial in character, more international in its outlook and, not least, better informed.

CHAPTER THREE

BANKING'S NEW FRONTIERS

Banking in the 19th century

For the major Western economies the nineteenth century was a period of massive expansion and also of frequent excitement. Europe's population, after nearly doubling in the eighteenth century, increased from an estimated 180-90 million in 1800 to over 450 million by 1914. That booming population was increasingly urban rather than landed; in Britain and Germany over half the population was city-based by the early twentieth century. The first industrial revolution transformed the British economy between 1750 and 1850, and by the mid-nineteenth century it had penetrated Germany, France, the Low Countries and the United States. By the end of the century industrialization was also the keynote of change in Spain, Italy, Sweden, Russia and Japan. Industrial output enlarged at an astonishing rate (world output of iron increased eight times over between 1860 and 1900), while national income and income per head leapt forward in all the industrializing nations.

Banking and finance followed, supported and in some instances led economic transformation in the nineteenth century. Unprepared and unrehearsed as banking may have been at the end of the eighteenth century, bankers were recognizable and even well-known figures on the economic stage a hundred years later. Likewise, other service industries – retailing, transport and communications, public utilities – came into more open view. Yet very few industries were involved in so many *dimen-*

The interior of Daiwa Europe, King William Street, London. The building, originally the head office of the Phoenix Assurance Company, was one of a series of important London sites chosen by the major Japanese banks in the 1980s.

sions of development as banking. In the nineteenth century banking continued and expanded its role in public finance; it was inextricably linked to the rise of industries and professions; it made contact with entirely new categories of customer and community; and it played a large part in extending the geographical boundaries of the world economy. Banks, no less than missionaries, adventurers and settlers, could be found at the frontiers of economic development.

In the area of public finance, banking solutions were adopted on a much broader front after 1800. On one hand, warfare and the maintenance costs of their empires placed a huge financial burden on the leading nation-states, thereby extending the need for banking management of state debts. On the other hand, the growing sophistication of trade and industry demanded greater order in national systems of currency and credit; control of the issue of banknotes emerged as a major preoccupation in nineteenth-century banking.

The Bank of England remained the most durable and prominent example of a national bank responsible for these aspects of public finance. After a century of sustaining state debts and managing the issue of notes, it was already setting the pattern for other national banking institutions. The Bank of Ireland, for example, was awarded similar privileges of joint-stock status when it was founded in Dublin in 1782.

Within the Bank of England itself, the

nation's conflict with revolutionary France brought a crisis of confidence in 1797. In the face of panic withdrawal of funds from country banks throughout England and Wales, the Bank was forced to suspend the payment of gold in exchange for its notes. For the duration of the Napoleonic Wars (and until 1819) paper currency was effectively inconvertible, a situation which conditioned the country into a preference for banknote transactions. Thereafter, the Bank diversified its role but its original and continuing responsibilities for government debt, the money market and the management of note-issue remained a telling influence on other banking systems.

Parallel institutions were also emerging in the other leading nation-states. In France Napoleon engineered the foundation of the state-regulated Banque de France in 1800. The Banque was a conversion of the Caisse des Comptes Courants, one of a group of note-issuing banks which had been promoted in Paris after the failure of the Caisse d'Escompte in 1796. The bank began life as a shareholders' concern with a capital of 30 million francs, but Napoleon insisted that his own government agents should take up shares and transfer their accounts. After 1805 the State also took over the appoint-

ment of the governor and his two deputies. A monopoly of note-issue, first awarded to the bank in 1803, but not complete until 1848, gave it the dominant role in French banking. However, it was not until later in the nineteenth century that the bank had anywhere near the same freedom as its English counterpart to expand the issue of banknotes.

In Germany attitudes to notes and paper currency were even more cautious. State-authorized issuing banks were not established in Bavaria until 1835 (the Baye-rische Hypotheken- und Wechselbank) and in Saxony until 1838 (the Bank of Leip-zig). When the Königliche Bank was reorganized as the Preussische Bank in 1846, its note-issue was restricted to 21 million thalers, though that limit was removed ten years later. After 1851 the Prussian prime minister was the head of the bank, and its senior officials were essentially state officials. This level of state control was maintained when the Reichsbank was founded as the federal successor to the Preussische Bank in 1875.

The other European nations did not adopt identical forms of banking monopoly, although the centralization of note-issuing was always a prime concern. In

Gold rushes were a significant but unpredictable factor in the world economy in the nineteenth century. In this sketch of about 1890, miners are seen bringing gold dust for weighing to G. A. Cook & Co. of Denver, Colorado.

Belgium the Banque Nationale de Belgique opened in 1851; it became the *de facto* monopoly when the other Belgian banks gave up their own note-issue in return for shareholdings in the new Banque Nationale. The French example had also been the inspiration behind the Nederlandsche Bank, which was formed as an issuing bank in 1814 and led to the demise of the Wisselbank in 1819.

These European models were significant influences on state banks in the industrializing nations of the later nineteenth century. In Japan early legislation to regulate banking was a variation of the American banking acts; however, the Bank of Japan, created by Matsukata, the Finance Minister, in 1882, then adapted the French and German pattern. A more distinctive feature was the creation of the Yokohama Specie Bank in 1880, a vehicle for financing Japan's foreign trade with state participation. In Russia the French influence on the banking scene was especially strong. The Russian State Bank, which had been founded as a

deposit-taking bank in 1860, was eventually given a monopoly of note-issue, similar to that of the Banque de France, in 1897. Although private accounts could be lodged with the bank, it was mainly an instrument of the state: by 1914 the Treasury's accounts comprised 70 per cent of the bank's total liabilities.

In contrast, the United States of America developed its own distinctive pattern of state banking. The charter of the first Bank of the United States (see p. 44) was not renewed when it expired in 1811, apparently as a result of pressure from the Bank's enemies in Congress. Nevertheless, when government debt mounted rapidly after the war with Britain in 1812–14, the search for a banking solution was renewed. The second Bank of the United States, launched in 1816, attempted to combine note-issuing, discounting and the management of government debt in the same style as its predecessor of 1791. Andrew Jackson, President between 1829 and 1837, doubted whether the US government had the con-

The Five Pound Note Office of the Bank of England in the mid-nineteenth century. This huge department was responsible for registering, 'pricking' and stamping bank notes when they had been paid.

Sir Thomas Lawrence's portrait of Sir Francis Baring, John Baring and Charles Wall, partners in Baring Brothers, London, at the end of the eighteenth century. The partners are seen consulting the ledger entry for Hope and Co. of Amsterdam, their closest allies in the development of international merchant banking.

'Dividend day at the Bank of England' by G. E. Hicks, 1850. The date for paying dividends on the Bank's stock became a set-piece event in Victorian London. Payment was not made unless stockholders and beneficiaries attended in person at the Dividend Office.

A paying teller or cashier and his customers at a New York deposit bank in 1890.

stitutional powers to sustain a national bank and withdrew the bank's privileges in 1836. The concessions – and the government's business – were transferred to banks authorized by individual States of the Union, leaving the Bank of the United States more or less stranded as a private bank until it became bankrupt in 1841. Thereafter, the issue of banknotes was left in the hands of private banks and by 1860 there were no less than 1,562 banks issuing notes.

In this climate there was little regulation, let alone management, of the government's own debts. The National Banking Act of 1863 at least clarified the duties of the Union and State governments. The Act distinguished between 'National' banks (joint-stock companies chartered and regulated by the Federal government) and 'State' banks (joint-stock banks, trust companies and property companies authorized by their own State governments). Under the new structure the number of note-issuing national banks multiplied rapidly from 500

in 1864 to over 2,000 in 1880. Meanwhile, State banks either gave up their note-issues or converted into National banks but they in turn multipled to nearly 4,500 in 1900. Not until 1913, however, was this huge banking population given its own central issuing bank. The Federal Reserve System created in that year introduced a central note-issue (operating through twelve Federal Reserve Districts) and required all National banks to place deposits with the Federal Reserve System. The appointment of the Board of Governors was in the hands of the President of the United States, matching the State's authority in the Banque de France and the Reichsbank.

Many of the leading nation-states had been slow or half-hearted in centralizing their banking needs. It was only in the later years of the nineteenth century and the early twentieth century that 'central' banks were a standard feature of the banking landscape. In the interim, the large financial needs of the major powers had revived or created new banking opportunities.

Nation-states had not lost their appetite for privately raised loans and international borrowing. Finance of this type was in a long tradition, stretching back to the Italian banking firms of the thirteenth and fourteenth centuries. That tradition had been extinguished neither by its attendant vicissitudes nor by the spread of broader-based banking institutions in the seventeenth and eighteenth centuries, and by the early nineteenth century a remarkable breed of privately owned international banks was showing that the trading of state debt was a viable – and survivable – business. These bankers, notable among whom were the Barings, Hopes and Rothschilds, were able to develop a multi-purpose, entrepreneurial role which was to be vital to financial markets over the next two centuries. The term 'merchant bank' was not used to describe these firms until the mid-nineteenth century (before then they preferred to describe themselves as 'merchants' or 'foreign bankers') but the description is used here to outline the origins of these banks.

The pre-eminent merchant bankers owed much to the economic power of Amsterdam and London. By the eighteenth century these centres had acquired the structures, attitudes and habits of international financial markets, and they were fertile ground for innovation and enterprise. In the Low Countries the firm of Hope and Co – Scots in origin – had been active in the commodity and bullion trades since the late seventeenth century. Even after Amsterdam's economic strength waned following the French invasion of 1795, Hope and Co was able to sustain its business by transferring to London for the duration of the French wars. There it consolidated its links with the firm of Baring Brothers, the dominant merchant bank in London at the beginning of the nineteenth century.

Barings had been founded in London in 1763, in tandem with the family's cloth trading business in Exeter. It became increasingly involved in banking operations from the 1770s, and in the 1780s it acted as the government's agent in buying supplies for the British army and in contracting for public loan subscriptions. By the turn of the century the firm was also arranging loans for the American government and for American trading partners. In 1803, in conjunction with Hopes, Barings found buyers for the $11 million loan which the United States government issued to pay for its purchase of Louisiana from the French. The Napoleonic wars gave Barings many more opportunities for financing foreign governments, and in the years that followed their clients included the State of Buenos Aires (from 1823), Upper Canada (1835), Chile (1844) and, in conjunction with Hopes, the Imperial Russian Government (from the 1840s).

Barings' leadership in merchant banking did not go unchallenged. In international finance their strongest rivals were the Rothschild interests in Germany, France and England. The founder of this remarkable dynasty, Meyer Amschel Rothschild, had begun business in Frankfurt in the mid-eighteenth century. Originally a general trader in textiles, antiques, medals and coins, he moved into bill dealing and (from 1764) became a factor or agent to the court of Hesse-Kassel. By the turn of the century he was the court's sole financial agent and the proceeds of this success enabled him to convert the business into the banking partnership of M. A. Rothschild & Sohne in 1810. The business spawned an international network of Rothschild banks headed by Meyer's sons – Amschel and Karl in Frankfurt, James and Salomon in Paris, and Nathan in London. Subsidiary firms were added in Vienna (1816) and Naples (1820), together with agencies in Europe and the Americas.

Of these interlocking interests, Nathan's business in England was the senior in age and in the size of its business. He had settled in England in 1798, subsequently building up a large textile export trade in Manchester. When the London firm of N. M. Rothschild was established in 1804, however, the emphasis was on banking

William IX, Elector of Hesse, entrusting securities to Meyer Amschel Rothschild (J. Oppenheim, Frankfurt, 1808). Rothschild's role as court factor was the foundation for an extraordinary and truly international dynasty of merchant banking.

Nathan Meyer Rothschild, by Richard Dighton, 1824. Rothschild founded the house of N. M. Rothschild in 1804 and within two decades he was acting as loan contractor for the British and Prussian governments. The Rothschild merchant banks throughout Europe were to acquire enormous political and financial influence between the Napoleonic Wars and the Crimean War.

Drawn Etch.ᵈ & Pubᵈ. by Richᵈ Dighton as the Act directs. May 1824

business, especially bullion dealing and contracting for government loans. In this merchant-banking role Rothschild captured British and international business, including a loan issue for Prussia in 1818 and the Rothschilds' first loan contract for the British government in 1819. The Frankfurt house was by then handling loans and debt negotiations for Austria and Prussia, while the Paris firm held a commanding position in the entangled finances of Spain and its American colonies; by 1904 the Rothschilds had been responsible for the staggering total of £1,300 million in loans to European nations. Their initiative had been especially decisive in enabling France to pay the indemnity 'fine' to Prussia after the war of 1871, and Rothschild intervention was also a turning point in Britain's purchase of a majority share in the Suez canal in 1875.

Although the Barings and Rothschilds could not be matched in the breadth and size of their dealings in state loans, this market became increasingly competitive as the nineteenth century progressed. In France *banque protestante* firms such as Perrégaux Laffitte & Cie and Hottinguer & Cie – both established by Swiss immigrants in Paris in the 1780s – were prominent in the negotiation of French reparation debts after 1815. In Germany the firm of Bethmann Brothers of Frankfurt had been lending to the Austrian court since 1754, and their neighbours and rivals Metzler Sohn & Co were bankers to both Bavaria and Prussia. Like the Rothschilds and other Jewish business dynasties in Germany, the Oppenheims, Seligmanns and Kaullas had been factors or financial agents to German courts in the late eighteenth century and in each case their banking firms developed state loan business in the early nineteenth century.

In London, Hambro's, founded by a firm of Danish merchants in 1839, specialized in loans to the Scandinavian countries and also acted for the Italian states; Kleinwort and Sons, who moved to London in 1830, cultivated strong links in eastern Europe.

Schroders, coming from Hamburg to London in 1804, had long-standing connections with Cuba, Chile and Peru, and they were to be the first international house to issue a loan for Japan in 1874. From the 1860s American private banks were also in the market for government loans and their successes included the US loan of 1874 (shared by the Rothschilds and others) and the French loan of 1870 (the first major issue managed by J. S. Morgan).

National and international government finance was a vital ingredient in the rise of these enterprises. The merchant banks of Europe and America were none the less active in a wide range of business. Some, like Barings, and Brown Shipley of Baltimore and Liverpool, sustained their original merchant role until late in the nineteenth century. Most houses relied heavily upon income from accepting bills from international traders; this business grew especially fast as Europe's trade with North America quickened between 1815 and 1835. Dealing in foreign exchange (and, in some cases, bullion) was a feature of many firms, especially when the telegraph came into use in the mid-nineteenth century. After the laying of the transatlantic cable in the 1870s the merchant banks in London and New York were able to generate useful income from 'arbitrage' – trading on differences between share prices in different markets. In all of these activities the merchant banks developed distinct specializations in different overseas markets, often reflecting their origins as trading houses or agencies.

Alongside their role in raising capital for governments, the merchant banks were also the springboard for new capital for the great railway and utilities projects of the nineteenth century. The most spectacular example was the Rothschilds' involvement in French, German and Austrian railway construction. The European Rothschild houses issued and subscribed for new railway stocks, to the extent that 10 per cent of all French railway capital was in Rothschild hands by 1848. Specialist firms also flourished during the boom period of railway building – notably Oppenheim & Cie of Cologne and, in Philadelphia, Drexel & Co (founded in 1838) and Jay Cooke & Co (established in 1861 but suspended in 1873). Perhaps the most remarkable European example of a railway specialist was the Brussels banker Baron Maurice de Hirsch, popularly known as 'Türkenhirsch', who on his own account acquired the concession for Turkish railways in 1869. The success of the deal brought Hirsch a huge fortune – thought to have been worth over £20 million at his death – and it also left the rich heritage of the Orient Express line from Paris to Constantinople, completed in 1888.

Although the British merchant banks were relatively less involved in railway finance, the London houses issued over $120 million in American and Canadian railway stocks between 1865 and 1890. Barings, who took nearly 30 per cent of this business, also participated in Russian railway stocks later in the century. Barings were, in addition, one of the few merchant banks to raise capital for industrial customers; they floated the massive £6 million issue for the brewers Arthur Guinness & Co in 1888.

The merchant banks of Europe and the United States were clearly opening up new financial territory by competing for business in a worldwide market. Their ambitions and connections contributed to the increasing internationalism of the financial community, but in other ways they were dealing with a relatively narrow section of economic life. The customers of merchant banks included governments and trading firms, railways and utilities – not forgetting the substantial business of dealing back and forth with other banks – but they did not cater for many private customers or for the smaller operators in industry, trade and the professions. It was the achievement of the nineteenth century to produce a pattern of banking which reached beyond these boundaries towards a wider spread of business and ownership, and towards a more visible role in the community. At the centre of that pattern was the development of joint-stock banking and branch banking.

Joint-stock banking, in which many shareholders could participate in a company with agreed rules of operation, was not the *invention* of the nineteenth century. The creditors of Italian city-states in the Middle Ages were in a sense 'shareholders' in public debt. In the seventeenth and eighteenth centuries the joint-stock form had also been adopted by the Amsterdam Wisselbank, the Bank of England and the three Scottish chartered banks. Yet it was only in the nineteenth century that shareholders' banks became a common feature of the financial scene and, eventually, dominated the banking market.

The joint-stock form of banking was already in place in the United States by 1800. The Bank of New York and the Bank of Boston (known as the First National Bank of Boston from 1864) had both been launched in 1784, while the Manhattan Company of 1799 was to emerge from its original business of water supply to become a banking corporation (now part of Chase Manhattan). In the first half of the nineteenth century a further 1,000 joint-stock banks were promoted in the United

The bank at Hackensack, New Jersey, in the 1870s. The signboard suggests that the bank was acting both as a national bank and as a savings institution.

The Stoppage of the Bank 1831, by Rolinda Sharples (1794–1838). A huge number of banks failed in England and Wales in 1825 and 1826, and Sharples probably chose the collapse of the Bristol Bullion Bank in 1825 as the model for this oil painting. She considered that bank failures were 'well suited to a great variety of expression.'

The joint-stock banks founded in England and Wales in the 1820s and 1830s were more ambitious in organization and buildings than their older competitors. This print shows the banking hall of the London and Westminster Bank, Lothbury, London, in 1845. The interior was designed by William Tite and the exterior was the work of Charles Cockerell.

States (excluding a significant number of savings banks which had appeared on the American scene since 1817).

Across the Atlantic at the beginning of the nineteenth century Scotland remained the stronghold of joint-stock banking in the shape of the three Edinburgh chartered companies. Joint-stock status was also chosen for the Commercial Bank of Scotland (1810), the National Bank of Scotland (1825) and the Aberdeen Town & County Bank (1825). In England and Wales, by contrast, the Bank of England had enjoyed exclusive status as a joint-stock bank since the early eighteenth century, forcing other banking enterprises to operate as small private partnerships. This in no way inhibited the proliferation of hundreds of private banks in London and the country, but the monopoly was increasingly inappropriate and the frailty of English private banking firms during the financial crises of 1815–16 and 1825 gave ammunition to its opponents. The

opposition campaign succeeded. The 1826 Banking Copartnerships Act brought the Bank of England's exclusive privileges to an end. The Act permitted the formation of joint-stock banks with any number of shareholders and with the right to issue their own notes, on condition that they were not based within sixty-five miles of London. Supplementary legislation in 1833 made away with the sixty-five-mile rule, although London-based joint-stock banks were prevented from issuing their own notes.

The response to the new legislation was rapid. Joint-stock banks were launched throughout England and Wales – usually as first-time companies but in some cases as conversions of old private banks – and within ten years over 100 of the new banks had been promoted, including the Midland (1836) and the main forerunners of the National Westminster Bank (1833–6). This sudden acceleration of banking enterprise and investment ran parallel to initiatives in

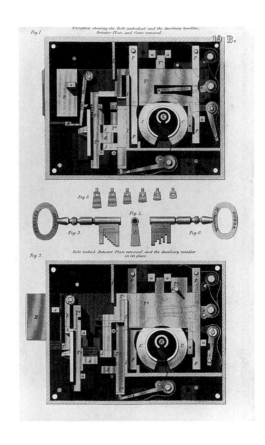

The growth of banking business in the nineteenth century brought a parallel expansion of the demand for security equipment. This advertisement published in 1850 reflects the strong competition between rival manufacturers of safes.

The 'lock controversy' at the Great Exhibition of 1851 was a confrontation between British and American lockmakers, each competing for a share of the lucrative banking market. This design shows the Permutating lock patented by Newell of New York.

Scotland, where Glasgow's promotions of the 1830s included the Union Bank of Scotland (1830), the Western Bank (1832), the Clydesdale (1838), and the City of Glasgow Bank (1839).

Domestic banking was a highly competitive business in the second and third quarters of the century, with the Bank of England joining the fray through new provincial branches, and the old private banks in London and the country refusing to give way to the new joint-stock concerns. Even in specialist areas of banking such as bill broking, the pace of competition sharply increased. From the 1820s discount houses emerged on the London scene, channelling bills of exchange to bankers and other institutions. After the largest discount house, Overend Gurney, failed in 1866, many of these intermediaries adopted joint-stock status. Thereafter they played a vital role as a buffer between the Bank of England and the banks, mainly by dealing in short-term funds.

None the less, it was primarily the joint-stock banks which took the lead in developing networks of branch banks throughout the country. The number of bank offices in the United Kingdom multiplied from about 1,700 in 1850 to 3,300 in 1875 and double that total by the end of the century. This commitment pushed banking into new territory: rural towns and villages, central and suburban areas of the industrial cities were given better access to basic banking services. Fierce competition between the banks also ensured that many communities enjoyed a choice of banks. For instance, a small country town such as Camelford in Cornwall could boast three banks in the 1880s; at the same time Haddington in Lothian, with a population of barely 4,000 people, had five Scottish banks competing for the town's business. Private customers could also turn to the growing numbers of savings banks. The pioneers of this movement included the Reverend Joseph Smith, whose Sunday Penny Bank opened at

The Bankers Clearing House in Lombard Street, originally exclusive to London private bankers, was used for the settlement of payments between banks. This sketch of 1847 gives the impression of a club atmosphere, but from the 1850s the entry of the London joint-stock banks gave the Clearing House a more comprehensive role in money transfer.

Any bank issuing notes needs to keep strict controls over the life-cycle of its bank notes. This print of 1872 shows the burning of old notes at the Bank of England.

Magnificent was not always synonymous with permanence in banking. The Bank of London, established in 1855, occupied this building in Threadneedle Street until the bank failed in 1866. Built in 1842, this interior had previously been the reading room of the Hall of Commerce.

A cathedral of banking: watercolour perspective based upon Joseph Goddard's design for the headquarters of the Leicestershire Banking Company, in 1874. The building is now the Granby Street Leicester office of Midland Bank.

Wendover in 1799; Mrs Priscilla Wakefield, founder of the Tottenham Benefit Bank in 1804; and Dr Henry Duncan of Ruthwell, Dumfries, 'the father of savings banks'. By 1904 approximately 400 savings banks were in existence, excluding many hundreds of offices of the Post Office Savings Bank (authorized by the government in 1861).

The British banks, private or joint-stock, continued to provide relatively restricted services to their home markets. They received deposits, settled payments, accepted and discounted bills, provided loans and overdrafts, and in some cases issued their own notes. Because in England and Wales their note-issues were restricted, from the mid-nineteenth century cheques became much more significant in the settlement of debts and payments. Annual turnover of cheques at the London Clearing House multiplied by more than five times to nearly £6 billion between 1840 and 1884. Thus, British banks attempted to supply basic services to a variety of customers in their home town or district. Those customers might include large manufacturing enterprises but they would also include small shopkeepers and purely personal accounts.

The adoption of joint-stock banking in Europe, in contrast, was often linked to specific tasks in industrial development. The honour of the first joint-stock investment bank belongs to the Société Générale de Belgique, chartered in 1822 to 'contribute to the progress, development and prosperity of agriculture, manufacturers, and commerce'. The Banque de Belgique, formed on the model of the Société Générale in 1835, entered the same field of industrial finance with the result that by 1840 no less than fifty-five joint-stock companies had been promoted by the two banks. In the main their support for industrial customers was based on mortgages, longer-term loans and direct shareholdings, and by 1860 the Société Générale could even claim that it held one fifth of the total capital of one billion francs in Belgian joint-stock companies.

Across the border in France the most successful of the Parisian private bankers (*la haute banque*) were already involved in funding canal construction in the 1820s. One of them, Jacques Laffitte, had also been canvassing plans for an industrial finance bank since 1825. When he inaugurated the Caisse Générale de Commerce et de l'Industrie in 1837 he promised his associates: 'my first step is to establish an ordinary bank, but I have in mind to convert it . . . into a real commercial and industrial bank'. Although this partnership venture perished in the financial upheavals of the 1848 revolution, Laffitte's ideas influenced joint-stock banking experiments after the mid-century. Of these the largest and most distinctive was the Société Générale de Crédit Mobilier, promoted in 1852 by the brothers Isaac and Émile Péreire. Joint-stock in form, its task was no less than the long-term financing of the French transport system and the principal heavy industries. By 1860

The Péreire brothers in the 1850s. Isaac and Emile Péreire founded the Société Générale de Crédit Mobilier in Paris in 1852. Although the bank eventually foundered, its close involvement with industry and transport has strongly influenced the development of 'universal' banking in continental Europe.

the Péreires' bank had financed over 10,000 kilometres of railway outside France and the brothers were threatening the supremacy in this field of the Rothschilds, their one-time employers.

To many in the world of finance the Péreires' initiative seemed to point the way forward. Even Joshua Bates, then the senior man at Barings, admitted that 'these sorts of Banks will get all the public loans', and gave support to certain Crédit Mobilier projects. Imitators of the French bank soon appeared throughout Europe. In Switzerland the creation of the Swiss Credit Bank by the energetic promoter Alfred Escher in 1856 laid the foundations of a strong banking tradition in Zurich. The *mobilier* example was followed in other Swiss cantons and in Italy and Spain. German bankers also saw a role for *mobilier* institutions. The Darmstädter Bank was founded on that basis in 1854, while the Disconto-Gesellschaft (opened originally as a deposit bank in Berlin in 1851) switched its business to the same pattern in 1865.

These new banks were the target of a remarkable counter-attack by the Rothschilds and their allies, coming together in 1856 as the Réunion Financière syndicate. The alliance used various devices to forestall or compete with the new banks, notably the promotion of the Österreichische Creditanstalt bank of Vienna in 1856. After a long political and business struggle, in 1864 the Rothschild syndicate was also permitted to create their own *mobilier*-type bank in France, the Société Générale pour Favoriser le Développement du Commerce et de l'Industrie en France. This tough response contributed to severe strain on the Crédit Mobilier in the financial crisis of 1857 and the eventual fall of the Péreire brothers in 1866. Although the remnants of the bank were then reconstructed, the Crédit Mobilier was only a shadow of its early promise and it was liquidated in 1902.

The Péreires had been preoccupied with long-term and almost immobile investment in industrial enterprise, to the neglect of traditional methods of payments and short-term credit. Their specialization had left no room for the private customer or for small business. To restore the balance, from the late 1850s the European financial community sought a middle way between the *mobilier* objectives and the joint-stock deposit banks of the United Kingdom. The Crédit Lyonnais, founded in Lyons by Henri Germain in 1863 and converted into a joint-stock company in 1872, was primarily a deposit bank with a network of country branches and agencies. The Paris-based Société Générale, after its initial launch as a *mobilier* bank in 1864, followed a similar path to the Lyons bank from the late 1860s. By the turn of the century the Crédit Lyonnais had over 200 branches in France and another 20 overseas, while the Société Générale operated nearly 350 branches in France. Likewise, in Germany there was a shift towards deposit banking on the British pattern. The Deutsche Bank and Commerz- und Disconto Bank were formed when company legislation was liberalized in 1870, and both were deposit banks with the emphasis on commercial rather than industrial finance. Thereafter, the German and Austrian banks emerged as the leading examples of 'universal' or 'mixed' banking combining short-term deposits with long-term investment banking and securities business.

Elsewhere in Europe, and beyond, the proliferation of banking owed much to the use of joint-stock form and branch networks. The pattern proved to be well adapted to industrializing nations such as Italy, Russia and Japan. In Italy a consortium of the largest German joint-stock banks was syndicating government loans in 1890, and the Germans subsequently played a strong hand in setting up Italy's largest joint-stock banks. In 1894 German, Swiss and Austrian banks combined in the formation of the Banca Commerciale Italiana in Milan in 1894. The new bank's nearest rival, the Credito Italiano of 1895, was essentially a relaunch of the Banca di Genova with the backing of the Nationalbank für Deutschland.

Coutts and Co. at 59 The Strand, Westminster, by John J. Farthing (1885). This London private bank was established in 1692, firmly in the goldsmith-banker tradition. It developed and maintained a reputation as a fashionable, aristocratic bank in the West End.

Bank customers of 1900 (at that date the children were visitors rather than customers). This drawing by F. D. Bedford for E. V. Lucas's *Book of Shops* is set in 'Pa's Bank' — a pun on Parr's Bank, a constituent part of the modern National Westminster Bank.

The earliest of the Russian joint-stock banks, the St Petersburg Private Commercial Bank, had been founded in 1864, and it was St Petersburg rather than Moscow which remained the centre of Russian finance throughout the century. By 1900 there were forty-three joint-stock banks in Russia, including many with German or Austrian connections. When, in 1887, Bismarck forced the German banks to curtail their Russian bank investments, the French banks were able to capture as much as half the foreign ownership of Russian banks by the early years of the twentieth century.

In contrast, banking development in Japan was firmly in the hands of the major *zaibatsu* – ancient family business empires such as the Mitsui, Mitsubishi and Sumitomo. The Mitsui, for instance, helped to promote the Dai-Ichi Bank of Tokyo, formed in 1873 as the first 'National' bank, and then created their own Mitsui Bank in 1876. The controlling influence of the *zaibatsu* in banks such as the Mitsui and Sumitomo (1895) was far removed from the shareholding structure of European joint-stock banks. Neither is there evidence of any Western investment in these banks. On the other hand, the Japanese banks adopted Western traditions in the development of their banking structure and operations. The Industrial Bank of Japan, launched in 1900, was in the *mobilier* mould of industrial finance. The singular figure of Alexander Allan Shand, who had learnt his banking in Scotland and England, was also a major influence on the Japanese system during his sojourn in Yokohama in the 1870s and afterwards as a manager of Parr's Bank in London, one of the principal banking agents of the government and railways of Japan.

The Western influence on newly developing countries was even more direct, principally in the dominions and colonies of the European empires. Britain, France, Germany and the other major powers exported not only capital for banking but also the organization, expertise and even the personnel of their banks at home. The British were especially prominent, both in their own territories and in non-aligned countries. Joint-stock banking in the Scottish tradition gained a foothold in Australia as early as 1817, when the Bank of New South Wales opened in Sydney, and in the same year the Bank of Montreal began business in Canada. In the case of the Bank of Montreal, British influence was also maintained by a large input of Scottish capital: ninety of the Bank's original subscribers were Scots.

A money-changer at Siout in Egypt in 1880, by X. A. Roth. Although colonial banks made significant progress in the Middle East, they did not displace the strong tradition of local exchange dealers.

Colonial banking then moved into a phase of intensive development in the second and third quarters of the century. Many of the leading banks promoted in British territories were London-based in their management and financed primarily by British shareholders. Front-rank examples were the Bank of Australasia in 1835 and the Bank of South Australia in 1837, the Bank of British North America in 1836, and the Colonial Bank, formed to operate in the key commercial region of the West Indies, in 1836. In the Indian sub-continent, where banking operations had been dominated by the East India Company and the commercial 'agency houses' until a series of failures between 1829 and 1832, a group of London-based joint-stock concerns now took up the pace of banking expansion. They included the Oriental Banking Corporation (1842), the Chartered Bank of India, Australia and China (1853) and the Mercantile Bank of India (1853), each with a network of branches in the sub-continent and in the major trading centres of the Far East.

The British influence on these overseas banks was further reinforced when, in 1846, all colonial joint-stock banks – whether based in London or in their home territories – became subject to supervision by the British government. Under this regime there was a huge investment in Anglo-colonial banks, of which sixty-eight were launched between 1853 and 1913. This generation of overseas banks included ambitious and successful ventures such as the Standard Bank of South Africa (1858) and the Hongkong and Shanghai Banking Corporation (1864). Under the leadership of the remarkable Thomas Jackson, chief manager for most of the period from 1876 to 1902, the Hongkong and Shanghai Bank took on a multiple role as agent to Imperial China, as banker to the colonial government and to other Eastern states, and as the principal commercial bank in the East.

The boom in overseas banking projects was not confined to British territories. Ventures such as the London and River Plate Bank (1862) were tied in with strong trading links in Argentina and Uruguay. Others, for example the Imperial Bank of Persia (founded in 1889 and now the British Bank of the Middle East), participated in public and railway finance for foreign states as well as in deposit banking.

The European banks were similarly active overseas, though not on the same scale as the imperial and international banks based in London. The Banque de l'Indo-Chine, established at Paris in 1875, played a dual role as an issuing bank and commercial bank in French colonies in the Indian Ocean and South-East Asia. Yet

The armed escort for West Coast Gold, New Zealand, in 1865. The escort was provided to move gold from the Westland mines to banks in Christchurch.

The Banque de l'Indo-Chine's office in Bangkok, Thailand, in 1908. This Paris-based bank was then represented throughout French Indo-China and also in Hongkong and Singapore.

The Bank of Japan, Tokyo, towards the end of the nineteenth century. This state bank, much influenced by European practice, had been established in 1882.

The waterfront at Hong Kong in about 1890. The head office of the Hongkong and Shanghai Banking corporation, designed by Bird and Palmer and completed in 1886, is visible on the left of the photograph.

French overseas banking was in the main *outside* the country's own empire. Russia was an important channel for investment (see p. 76) and French-owned banks were also active in Latin America, Spain and the Near East. For example the Banque Impériale Ottomane was primarily a French initiative when in 1863 it began business at Constantinople and at branches throughout the Ottoman Empire.

Towards the end of the century, German banks also made a determined entry into overseas business. Fingers were burned by the failure in 1885 of the Deutsch-Belgische La Plata Bank, formed in 1872 to support German and Belgian trade with Uruguay and Argentina, but the Deutsche Überseeische Bank of 1886 was altogether more successful in South America. The venture was sponsored by the Deutsche Bank and based in Berlin, and by 1905 all the major German banks were sharing in South American subsidiaries. Inter-bank co-operation was also important in the creation of the Deutsch-Asiatische Bank at Berlin and Shanghai in 1889, allowing the new bank to play an expansive role in German development of the Shantung province of China.

The overseas projects of European bankers and investors relied heavily upon capital and political support from their home markets. Even so, their progress would have been impossible without the frontier spirit in which overseas bankers tackled their work. Thousands of young European bankers – the Scots were one of the largest groups – travelled in the steps of the first settlers and traders, attempting to provide a service in the most primitive conditions. To run a branch network in the relative comfort of a European community was not at all the same challenge as operating branches and agencies in uncharted areas of South-East Asia or Africa. The challenge confronting home-grown banks was equally strong. The Australian branch banks of the nineteenth century, for example, were a triumph over the obstacles of communication and transport. Similarly the North American banks were exposed to all the difficulties of long-distance business, including the skirmishes and lawlessness which placed banks and bank robberies in the literature and culture of the American West. Wells Fargo of San Francisco, originally the 'Express Company' of carriers rather than bankers, made the transition into banking by overcoming these only too real hurdles to financial development. The risks were lampooned in a notice

issued by a Wyoming bank after a series of shooting incidents in 1906:

> Patrons thinking an error has been made are requested not to shoot the cashier before making investigation. Strangers must enter the bank holding their hands above their heads or they will be fired on by staff. Deposits of persons killed on the premises remain the property of the bank. The bank will not be responsible for lost guns or bowie knives. Persons desirous of transacting business quickly will please remember that shooting out the light tends to delay rather than to expedite the work of the staff. This bank will not be responsible for the funeral charges of persons killed on the premises of the bank.

But increasingly during the nineteenth century the main danger had come from commercial and financial crisis. Periods of severe stress, such as the mid-1820s in Britain and South America, and the late 1830s and late 1850s throughout Europe and the United States had decimated the population of private and joint-stock banks. In some cases, that stress was exacerbated by fundamental weaknesses in banks themselves – the reckless over-extension which led to the failure of the Agricultural & Commercial Bank of Ireland and the Northern and Central Bank in 1836–7, the wild investments which ruined the London discount house of Overend Gurney in 1866, the crookedness which led to the collapse of the City of Glasgow Bank in 1878, or the wilful fraud that overwhelmed a number of savings banks late in the century. In other cases, the crises affecting banks were part of more generalized economic difficulty. A severe squeeze in the American bond market brought an end to the Boston house of Jay Cooke and Co in 1873, and a stock-market collapse also led to the downfall of the Union Générale of Paris in 1882. One of the most serious upheavals of this kind was the Australian banking crisis of 1893, when a long period of heavy investment in Australia culminated in a speculative boom in land prices. The boom collapsed in April and May 1893, driving three Australian banks into liquidation. Another thirteen banks, with total liabilities of over £100 million, were forced to suspend payments for the duration of the crisis.

These examples are only part of the long roll-call of failures and crises which affected the banking community in the nineteenth century. Yet the century also saw serious progress in coping with banking disasters or reducing their impact. This was partly

The Union Bank of Australia's branch at Charleston, New Zealand, in 1871. In 1840 the Union Bank had been the first bank to open in New Zealand, and this early photograph captures the pioneer style of banking throughout Australasia.

Wells Fargo's original business as stage-coach express carriers included contracts for delivering cash and payments. Banking and exchange services were added in 1852.

Banking in frontier territory: the wood-built bank of Stebbins, Post and Co. at Deadwood, Dakota, USA in about 1877.

Reward notice posted after the unsuccessful raid by Jesse James and the Younger brothers on a bank at Northfield, Minnesota, in 1876.

REWARD!
- DEAD OR ALIVE -

$5,000.00 will be paid for the capture of the men who robbed the bank at

NORTHFIELD, MINN.

They are believed to be Jesse James and his Band, or the Youngers.

All officers are warned to use precaution in making arrest. These are the most desperate men in America.

Take no chances! Shoot to kill!!

J. H. McDonald,
SHERIFF

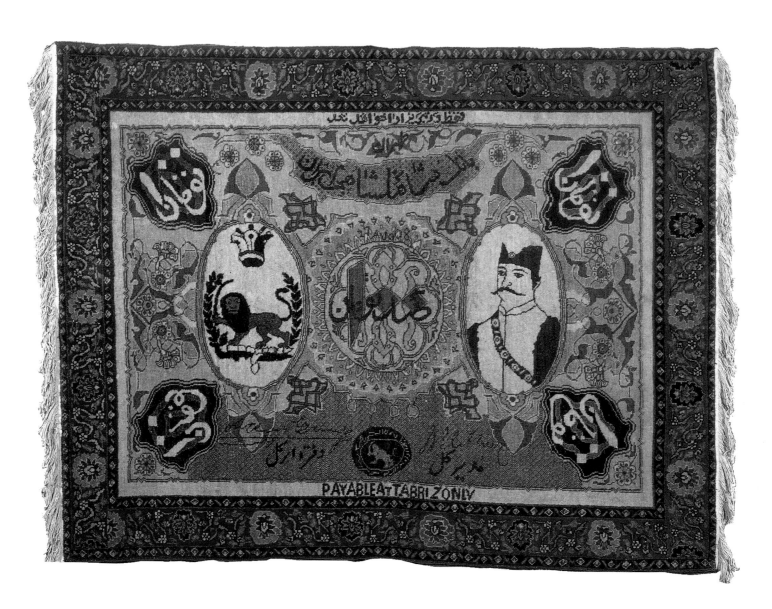

A Persian carpet made for the Imperial Bank of Persia in about 1900. The pattern of the carpet is modelled on a bank note of the Tabriz branch of the Imperial Bank.

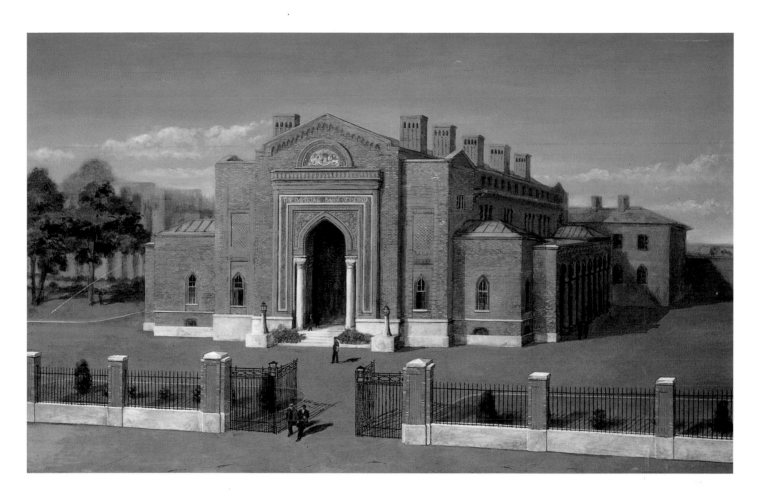

The Imperial Bank of Persia, Tehran, in about 1930. This London-based bank had been established as the state bank of Iran in 1889. Its links with Iran ended in 1952 but, renamed the British Bank of the Middle East in 1952, it sustained an important role in middle eastern banking. Since 1960 the British Bank of the Middle East has been a subsidiary of the Hongkong and Shanghai Banking Corporation.

'Run on a bank' from *Harper's Magazine*, 1890. As the telegraph and telephone came into wider use at the end of the nineteenth century, news or rumours of a bank failure would spread very quickly. In this fictional portrait, investors and depositors throng the doors at their bank; panic withdrawals of cash could occasionally overwhelm a bank where no real danger had existed beforehand.

The New York Clearing House Association in 1887. The Association had been founded in the 1850s and it acted as the clearing point for cheques and other inter-bank payments. By 1900 the Clearing House was handling transactions totalling over fifty billion dollars each year.

The banking hall of the First National Bank, Wichita, Kansas in about 1890. Most American banks of this period maintained separate counters for receiving cash, paying out (withdrawals) and telling out coins and notes.

the result of an upgrading of techniques, professional standards and education; institutes of bankers were launched in Scotland (1874), England (1879), the United States, and Australia. Legislation governing the composition and conduct of banks was also a factor. Banking was an increasingly rule-bound business in the nineteenth century, particularly in the United States with its National Banking Act of 1863. In the United Kingdom, after the City of Glasgow Bank failure of 1878 had exposed damaging weaknesses in joint-stock bank regulations, the reform of limited liability in 1880 was designed to give greater security to shareholders and customers of British banks, while the Bills of Exchange Act of 1882 was a landmark in standardizing the practice of banking.

By the end of the century the banking scene had also acquired experience and expertise in dealing with moments of crisis. Warfare and political turmoil were more easily absorbed – and even indeed discounted – by the international banking network than had been possible in the previous two centuries. When crisis was unavoidable, the banking structure was also better equipped to respond. The role of

national or 'central' banks was crucial at such moments. As early as 1837 the Bank of England agreed to support the Liverpool house of William and James Brown (later Brown Shipley) at a moment of panic and confusion in Anglo-American trade. Again, in 1890, the Bank of England headed a subscription list of British bankers in guaranteeing the debts of Baring Brothers, which was in danger of succumbing to a huge financial exposure in Argentina.

In these cases the notion of a 'lender of last resort' was emerging, fashioned by the lessons of coping with crises and panics. The value of formal and informal co-operation between banks was also better understood, whether through associations of banks or through inter-bank agreements on competition and working conditions. The result was a greater cohesion and community of interests in national and international banking. With bankers continually entering new territories of business, this stability helped to sustain public confidence at home and abroad. It was also an essential background for the very large banking institutions which were already emerging to dominate the financial scene in the early twentieth century.

CHAPTER FOUR

THE BIG BATTALIONS

The banking world from 1900 to 1950

This startling interior is now the entrance hall to Lloyds Bank's Law Courts branch in The Strand, London. It was originally a club and restaurant, designed by Wimble and Cuthbert in 1883 with the entrance decorated in Doulton tiles. Lloyds converted the building into a bank in 1895, shortly after the acquisition of the old private banks of Praeds and Co. of Fleet Street (established 1802) and Twining and Co. of The Strand (established 1824).

By the end of the nineteenth century the world-wide banking industry was crowded with an extraordinary range of types of business. This variety was in many ways a sign of strength, showing that banking business could be adapted to special needs and situations. Yet it also introduced a strong element of fragmentation into the financial community. By 1900 the wide dispersal of skills and resources may already have left some categories of banks too small and too fragile to live with sweeping change in economic and business affairs. Efforts to overcome this potential weakness were to be an early and important theme of twentieth-century banking development.

The proliferation of banks was obvious enough from the sheer number of companies and firms claiming to offer banking services. In the United Kingdom the *Bankers' Almanac* in 1900 listed nearly 250 private and joint-stock banks, ranging from conventional deposit banks to discount houses and merchant banks. Its roll-call for the 'principal, foreign and colonial banks' reached 1,025. London, undoubtedly the world's largest and busiest banking centre at the beginning of the century, was equipped with no less than 722 bank offices; the total for the United Kingdom as a whole was 6,600, not including the hundreds of outlets of the savings banks and the Post Office Savings Bank. In number, if not in variety, the population of American banks by 1900 was even larger, with nearly 4,400 State banks, 3,700 National banks and

about 1,000 savings banks. By 1914 these totals had more than doubled.

This abundance of banks made the industry a more obvious, visible feature of modern society. By 1900 the head offices and branches of banks (especially the larger deposit banks) were landmarks of city-centres, fast-expanding suburbs, market towns, staging posts and smaller settlements. The appearance of these buildings was often grand and elaborate, as the architecture of banks was one of the few ways in which they were prepared to advertise themselves. At corner sites or in main streets these edifices could rival town halls and other public buildings in terms of their prominence and prestige, and some of the larger banks were already employing architects who specialized in bank design. As a result banks increasingly adopted standard design features for their buildings and fittings – a trend which gathered pace later in the century.

At the outset of the twentieth century these buildings reflected bankers' eagerness to give a public impression of solidity and permanence. They also signalled the growing significance of banking on the employment scene. Although numbers for the industry as a whole are not certain, by 1900 the population of the world's banking staff was counted in hundreds of thousands rather than in thousands. In the United Kingdom alone, the payrolls of individual banks suggest that the total banking work-force may have reached between

30,000 and 40,000 at the turn of the century. This was only a small proportion of the great army of commercial clerks in the major economies – that breed of counting-house commuters typified by Mr Pooter in *Diary of a Nobody*. Unlike many of their contemporaries, however, bank clerks enjoyed comparatively good working conditions and prospects. Formal salary scales were increasingly common by 1900; in England and Wales the level of salaries ranged from £40 for a junior apprentice to £350 for a country branch manager, and to the dizzy heights of over £2,000 for a general manager. Pension schemes and provident funds were also part of the employment package in the major banks. Even if career progression could be grindingly slow for the majority of clerks, prospects were much improved by the opening of new branch offices at home and abroad.

The competition for bank appointments was fierce, as *The Bankers' Magazine* had complained in 1892:

The market is well stocked with bank clerks – overstocked. Put an advertisement in the paper –

BANK CLERKS WANTED
COMMENCING SALARY £50. MUST
HAVE GOOD KNOWLEDGE OF BOOK-
KEEPING, FRENCH, GERMAN,
SHORTHAND. APPLY 'BANKER' C/O
DAILY TELEGRAPH

and we have no hesitation in saying that there will be a couple of hundred, ay, three hundred applications. Knock off some of the qualifications and reduce the salary to £20, and you will find almost an equal number of aspirants.

These magnificent bronze gates were designed by W. D. Caroe for the Adelphi Bank, Liverpool, in 1892. The Adelphi Bank was a constituent part of Martins Bank but the building is now a branch of the Co-operative Bank.

Banks responded to this competition for jobs by introducing entrance examinations and by encouraging their employees to obtain professional qualifications. Thus, between 1890 and 1914 the Institute of Bankers, with British and overseas members, saw a fivefold increase to a total of 10,500 members and a twentyfold increase in the number of candidates for its professional examinations.

In the banking industry of the early twentieth century the majority of this large work-force was employed by the leading commercial banks. State or central banks operated with relatively small numbers of staff, the Bank of England being the largest of its kind with a staff of about 700. Similarly, the merchant banks varied in size from 100 for a leading house such as Barings to a handful of clerks for new entrants into the business. In contrast, the deposit-taking banks with their networks of branches were being transformed by amalgamations and alliances, and at the outbreak of the First World War the larger

companies were each employing several thousand bank staff.

In the United Kingdom this process of amalgamation and concentration had been under way since the 1880s, initially through the acquisition of private banks and small joint-stock banks by larger regional joint-stock banks, and subsequently through the amalgamation of regional banks by London-based banks with nationwide representation. The banking landscape altered substantially as a result, so that by 1900 the ten largest banks accounted for over 40 per cent of the United Kingdom's bank deposits. This leading group included Lloyds and the Midland (both founded in Birmingham but relocated in London in 1885 and 1891 respectively), the National Provincial Bank, Barclays (an alliance of twenty private banks incorporated under the Barclays flag in 1896) and the London and County Bank.

A comparable process of concentration was also affecting the German and American banking industries. In America the most striking feature of banking business

The banking hall of an unidentified American bank in about 1900. Elaborate and sometimes forbidding counters and screens were by then a feature of branch banks throughout the world.

The manager's room at Barclays Bank, 160 Piccadilly, London. In contrast to the plain mahogany panelling of most bank interiors, the rich oriental treatment of this room had been commissioned originally in 1922 for the London office of Wolseley Motors.

Barclays Bank, 160 Piccadilly, London. The ornate treatment of this banking hall is the legacy of the architect William Curtis Green. Green had designed the ground floor as a showroom for Wolseley Motors in 1922, but when the carmaker failed in 1926 the building was acquired by Barclays. Green was employed to make the conversion from showroom to branch bank.

was the ascendancy of New York. Practically one quarter of American bank deposits were placed with New York banks by 1909, and the New York Clearing House handled 60 per cent of the cheque clearings. The city was also the home territory of the largest national banks – notably the National City Bank, the three major trust companies (the Guaranty Trust, Bankers' Trust and Manufacturers' Trust), and the powerful group of private banks led by J. P. Morgan & Co, Kuhn Loeb & Co and Brown Brothers.

In Germany the concentration of banking power centred on Berlin, from where a group of eight banks, headed by the Deutsche Bank, Disconto-Gesellschaft and Dresdner Bank, remorselessly strengthened their balance sheets by the acquisition of small provincial and private banks. By 1911 over fifty had been taken over, and a further thirty were then acquired by subsidiaries of the Disconto-Gesellschaft. Small banks still survived in large numbers, but even here the large banks dominated the position by collaborating in loans or by taking shares in the smaller regional banks. In this sense the German banks were pioneers of 'group' banking. Interwoven shareholdings gave the largest banks access to the resources of subsidiary companies, most obviously in the alliances which the Deutsche Bank and Disconto-Gesellschaft formed with regional banks before 1911.

In France, in contrast, concentration in the banking industry owed more to the extension of branches than to amalgamations and alliances. The three giants of the industry – the Crédit Lyonnais, the Société Géńerale and the Comptoir National d'Escompte – were represented through a total of 1,150 offices by 1908. Their aggregate deposits of 4,360 million francs loomed over the total of only 860 million francs accumulated by the largest provincial and regional banks.

The concentration of banking business into the hands of very large commercial banks had followed different patterns and different timetables in the leading indus-

Wall Street, New York, in 1894. At a period of strong economic growth, Wall Street was already the hub of financial influence in the United States.

trial nations. Yet by the early years of the century the process had produced a generation of banks which were comparable in size and resources (Table 4). By 1908 the Deutsche Bank was the largest of the class in terms of total assets and third in total deposits (the measure which was most often used in the first half of the century). The major French and American banks, too, were well represented amongst the ten largest asset-holding banks. The main characteristic of this ranking was nevertheless the number of front-ranking banks which were British or in the British sphere of influence. The amalgamation period in British banking had given Lloyds first place in terms of deposits; with 560 branches it also had the largest number of offices in the leading group. The strength of the London banks was deep-seated, as no less than nine of the top twenty banks by total assets were based in the capital; another three in the top rank (the Bank of New South Wales, the Bank of Montreal and the Hongkong and Shanghai Banking Corporation) were empire-based.

Contemporary bankers explained the trend towards very large banking units mainly in terms of the need to keep pace with the expansion of industrial companies, public utilities, and municipal bodies. These major customers of the banks required payments services and borrowing on a scale which was beyond many local or specialized banks. The motives for expansion and amalgamation were not always so simple, however. The need to give a public impression of size and stability was also a factor in the aftermath of the bank failures of the nineteenth century. Moreover, the search for new business influenced many banks' efforts to expand, especially when they found that business in their original territory was stagnant or declining in the face of new competition.

Personalities and politics also made a serious contribution to the development of the front-ranking banks. Many of the largest units were dominated by individuals who were as skilled in merger negotiations and in planning corporate expansion as they were in the banking business. In the United States, John Pierpoint Morgan (1837–1913) was the outstanding example of this interesting breed. He was not only the senior partner in the private banking house of J. P. Morgan but he was also a key figure in the First National Bank of New York from the 1890s and principal shareholder in the National City Bank (from 1907). From this platform Morgan co-ordinated and controlled industrial empires such as the gigantic United States Steel Corporation and the Northern Pacific Railroad.

Morgan was evidently as powerful at moments of financial tension. During the gold crisis of 1895 he led a syndicate of American bankers in halting the outflow of gold from the United States, and again in 1907 – after the failure of a massive speculation in copper triggered a run on the banks – he took a vital role in preventing the collapse in confidence. This crisis, and Morgan's proposals for handling the challenge, were important factors in the creation of the American Federal Reserve system in 1913 (see p. 60). By the time of his death in 1913, Morgan's own bank was represented on the boards of directors of 112 companies, including the National City Bank, the Bankers' Trust Company and the Guaranty Trust Company.

In Europe the great personalities of banking expansion had a similar breadth of interests and influence. Georg von Siemens (1839–1901), the outstanding character in the formative years of the Deutsche Bank, shared the same ambitious approach to industrial development as well as banking. In the United Kingdom Sir Edward Holden (1848–1919) not only converted the Midland Bank from a relatively low-ranked country business to the largest bank in the world by 1918, but was also the financial adviser to some of the largest British industrial and commercial conglomerates.

The expansive style of such banking leaders did not go unchallenged. In the United States and the United Kingdom there was considerable public and official disquiet over the possibility that the major banks were acting as 'money trusts', dividing up the available business between themselves and eliminating fair competition. Although the 1912 'money trust' hearings before the House of Representatives could not produce conclusive evidence that such a trust was in existence, there was little doubt that the major banks under investigation (including Morgan, the First National, and the National City Bank) were the motive power in the concentration of banking. Similarly, in the United Kingdom the Colwyn Committee – formed in 1918 to examine a renewed surge in banking amalgamations – disliked some fea-

Olaf Guldbransson's cartoon of John Pierpoint Morgan's 'mountain of gold' in 1916. In the early years of the century the house of Morgan was a mighty influence on American government and industry as well as in banking.

This anonymous cartoon of about 1910, muddled though it may be, is a reminder that pass books were provided for all current accounts until well into the twentieth century.

tures of the merger movement but had to be content with a 'gentleman's agreement' in which the major banks would not attempt further acquisitions without the approval of the Treasury.

A striking feature of these debates over 'money trusts' was the virtual admission that the major commercial banks played too valuable a role in public policy to be curtailed in their ambitions. In the decade before the First World War this public role had included intervention at moments of crisis, such as Morgan's rescue act in 1907, or Holden's lead in preventing the failure of the Yorkshire Penny Bank in 1911 and 1915. It was also clear that bankers themselves viewed the growth of their business in the context of contemporary international politics. British bankers in particular repeatedly described their expansion as a necessary response to the power of German banking capital and the continuing struggle for supremacy in overseas markets. The scramble for representation in Russian banking was a colourful reflection of this international rivalry. In St Petersburg and Moscow the agents of French, German, British and American banks all jostled for position during the boom in investment in Russia between 1905 and 1914. The result was that by 1916 as much as 45 per cent of the capital of Russia's ten largest banks was in foreign hands.

These international rivalries in finance were brought into sharp and ugly focus at the outbreak of the First World War in August 1914. Within hours of the declaration of war the senior bankers on both sides were entangled in negotiation with their governments. Political leaders relied heavily upon banking advice both for the finance of the war effort and for the more mundane task of sustaining currency and payments. 'If you saw the length of the faces of those who know,' wrote Patrick Shaw-Stewart, partner in Barings, 'you would realize this is one of the most terrific things London has been up against since finance existed.' Shaw-Stewart did not live to see the outcome; like so many of his generation in the City of London, he was killed on the Western Front.

The strains of war quickly led to a complete dislocation of the established pattern of international finance. All the major belligerent countries except the United Kingdom were forced to abandon the gold standard, in effect giving up the principle that banknotes were convertible into gold and severely restricting the export of gold.

Bank failures were always cruel in their consequences, especially when small savers were the victims. The protests and grief of customers are dramatized in this illustration of the stoppage of the National Penny Bank, Westminster, London, in 1914.

In 1911 the Birkbeck Bank, High Holborn, London, failed with total liabilities of over twelve million pounds. The deposits were eventually compensated when the business was taken over by the London County and Westminster Bank.

In the First World War all the combatant nations relied heavily upon war loans and public subscriptions. The major banks had an important role both as investors and as collecting points. This advertisement, the work of Georges Redon, was published by the Societé Générale of Paris to appeal for subscriptions to national loans.

Even in Britain the Bank of England was permitted to step up the issue of notes without increasing its gold reserves. As a result there was a huge increase in the volume of banknotes in circulation. In the United Kingdom the total nearly doubled to £383 million by mid-1918, excluding £299 million of 'currency notes' issued by the Treasury. Similarly, in Germany the note circulation shot up from 2.4 billion marks in June 1914 to nearly 19 billion marks by the end of the war.

Part of this expansion of money supply reflected the high levels of wartime inflation. For the banks there was also a serious impact on the volume of cash handled and on the level of deposits held by the banks. In Germany the major banks saw a fourfold increase to 19.7 billion marks between 1914 and the end of 1918, while in Britain total bank deposits doubled to over £2.2 billion between 1914 and 1919.

In contrast, the merchant banks, with the exception of the American houses, suffered a period of slack business; the interruption of international commerce and traditional acceptance and issuing business left many of these banks on a care and maintenance basis. On the London market, moreover, those houses with strong German linkages

disappeared from the scene.

Central and commercial banks on both sides of the conflict were closely involved in the negotiation of international credits to sustain their governments' war efforts. The overriding theme of these negotiations was the transformation of the United States from a debtor nation to the world's largest creditor. At the outbreak of war European assets in the United States had been worth about $7 billion net; five years later the position had reversed, with American claims on Europe reaching about $12 billion.

Whether in the sale of European investments to American buyers or in the raising of new loans to the belligerents, the American banking houses performed a large neopolitical role. In the first part of the war J. P. Morgan & Co handled all the dollar loans to the British and French – notably the $500 million Anglo-French loan of 1915, in which Morgans headed a consortium of sixty-one New York banks and trust companies. Further heavy lending to the Allied powers was organized by Morgans and their New York partners in the American Foreign Securities Company over the next

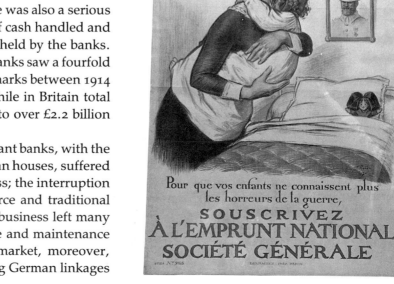

Pour que vos enfants ne connaissent plus les horreurs de la guerre,

SOUSCRIVEZ
À L'EMPRUNT NATIONAL
SOCIÉTÉ GÉNÉRALE

The *Black Horse* mosaic roundel by Gilbert Bayes in the banking hall of Lloyds Bank, Lombard Street, London. The date 1677 echoes an early reference to the Black Horse sign in Lombard Street; Lloyds Bank, which had previously used the beehive symbol, inherited the Black Horse sign when it acquired the firm of Barnetts, Hoares, Hanbury and Lloyds in 1884.

The banking hall of Lloyds Bank's head office in Lombard Street, London, designed by Sir John Burnet and Partners, and Campbell, Jones, Sons and Smithers. Lloyds had first moved from Birmingham to London in 1885. The completion of the Lombard Street headquarters in 1930 was part of a massive rebuilding programme by the major British banks in the interwar period.

two years; by April 1917, when the United States finally entered the war, the American banks had negotiated over $2.1 billion in loans to the Allied powers and had handled the purchase of over $3 million of American securities from the Europeans.

If the Great War had shaken the foundations of international finance, in Russia those foundations gave way altogether. The finance of the Russian war effort was already dependent upon Allied credit, and European investment remained a large factor in Russian production and banking. The revolutions of 1917 and Russia's withdrawal from the war more or less wiped out the value of those credits and investments, and the new Bolshevik government thereafter refused to honour debts incurred under the Tsarist regime; France, for example, lost nearly $4 billion in Russian assets.

These claims became an unusual feature of Western banks' balance sheets for many years after the Revolution. For instance, it was another seventy years before Anglo-Soviet claims and counter-claims arising from the Revolution could be regularized.

The wartime dislocation of international finance was paralleled by turmoil in the staffing and management of the banks. In the United Kingdom, for example, about 18,000 bankers joined the services during the war; they included a special 'Bankers' Battalion', which was raised in London in 1915 and later saw action in France and Italy. The departure of so many staff left a serious shortage of skill to cope with the rapid expansion of business in the war years. In response, the banks recruited large numbers of women and junior staff to fill the gaps. Whereas the 1911 British cen-

Cox and Co. of London, established in 1758 and acquired by Lloyds Bank in 1923, developed a long tradition as bank agents for the British armed services. This photograph at the end of the First World War shows the department handling Royal Air Force officers' banking accounts.

The pattern of banking employment was irrevocably altered by the recruitment of women, especially during the First World War. This group of Girl Guides worked as messengers for Cox and Co. of Charing Cross, London, in the latter stages of the War.

sus showed that only 1 per cent of bank staff were women, by the end of the war a large commercial bank such as Lloyds employed as many as 3,300 women, 29 per cent of its total work-force. When demobilized servicemen returned to banking, many of the women who had taken their place remained in the industry. Initially this created an overcrowded profession but in the 1920s and 1930s the upward trend in the number of women bankers was maintained.

The financial and banking consequences of the First World War, as in so much of twentieth-century life, were profound. The most obvious legacy was the complex web of international debts (principally the Allied debts to the United States) and the reparations imposed upon Germany and her allies under the terms of the Peace of

Versailles in 1919. The level of those reparations was quoted by the Reparations Commission at the huge sum of 132 billion marks. A settlement was delayed until 1929, when the 'Young Plan', devised by a conference of international experts, produced a new formula for debt repayments and the dismantling of post-war impositions on Germany. Under the auspices of the plan, Germany's remaining debts were reduced to 34.5 billion marks and offset by international loans of 800 million marks and $300 million dollars.

The disentangling of Allied debts and German reparations was not only a question of international financial policy. It was also a highly sensitive issue for the world of banking. Leading figures such as J. P. Morgan Junior, Paul Warburg (of Kuhn Loeb), Émile Moreau (Governor of the Bank of

The painted facade of the Union Bank of Switzerland branch in Einsiedeln, Switzerland

The Park Lane, London branch of Barclay's Bank. The magnificent gothic design of Stanhope House was the work of W.H. Romaine-Walker in 1898. Originally occupied by R.W. Hudson, the soap manufacturer, the building has been a Barclays branch since 1952.

France) and Lord Revelstoke (of Barings) played a part in the initiatives which led up to the Young Plan of 1929. The Young Plan itself was to leave a permanent mark on banking history in the shape of the Bank for International Settlements (BIS), established at Basle in 1930. The central banks of Belgium, France, Germany, Italy, Japan and the United Kingdom all participated in the BIS and were later joined by the central banks of the Netherlands, Sweden, Switzerland and a consortium of American commercial banks. The work of the BIS – the first truly international collaboration in banking – included the transfer of reparation payments and the settlement of other international debts.

The choice of a Swiss location for the BIS was especially appropriate. Since the end of the First World War, Swiss banks had been the haven for international payments in gold and currency, and the national traditions of neutrality and confidentiality meant that the Swiss banks attracted a huge inflow of savings and investments. Indeed, between the wars the secrecy of bank transactions was given more legal force in Switzerland than in any other banking centre. While the rest of Europe was subject to official controls on the movement of money, the banks of Zurich, Basel and the other Swiss cantons were given a massive vote of confidence by private and corporate customers throughout the world.

While the governments and banking establishments of the major powers grappled with the legacies of the Great War, the period between 1918 and 1939 proved to be full of contrasts and contradictions within the banking community. On one hand, these were years of solid progress in the spread of banking business. On the other, the inter-war period confronted bankers with the twin challenges of crisis and recession, challenges which were to enlarge the overlap between banking and government policy.

Many of the the strong themes of pre-war banking development were maintained after 1918. The concentration of business

even gained momentum during and immediately after the war. In the United Kingdom a small group of banks (the 'Big Five' of Barclays, Lloyds, Midland, National Provincial and Westminster) shared about 63 per cent of all bank deposits when the main phase of amalgamations drew to a close in 1918. Concentration through mergers was also a factor in post-war Germany, where a series of bank weddings culminated in the amalgamation of the Deutsche Bank and

In the early 1920s Germany experienced a period of hyper-inflation. The huge numbers of bank notes for quite small transactions were bundled into tea-chests instead of cash registers.

The rush for new bank notes isued by the Banque de France in 1920. Public confidence in bank notes has been a *sine qua non* of banking systems for three centuries.

the Disconto-Gesellschaft in 1929. The assets of the merged bank reached 5.5 billion marks, a total which dwarfed the balance sheets of competitors such as the Dresdner (2.5 billion marks) and the Commerz- und Privat-Bank (1.9 billion marks).

Likewise, in America bank amalgamations were an ever-present feature of the 1920s: between 1919 and 1929 the staggering total of 4,177 mergers spelled the end of independence for nearly 8,000 banks. Amongst the big players the Guaranty Trust acquired the National Bank of Commerce in the summer of 1929. More spectacularly still, during 1930 A. P. Giannini consolidated his banking interests under the new title of the Bank of America; at the time the group ranked as the fourth largest bank in the United States. The outcome of this phase of concentration was the three-fold increase in the major banks' share of business. By 1930 as much as 13 per cent of total bank assets was held by the six largest of the American banks – Chase National,

At first women in banking were placed mainly in 'back-office' jobs. These bank clerks were photographed in the traditional office surroundings of Cox and Co.'s Stock Office in about 1919.

National City, Guaranty Trust, Bankers' Trust, Irving Trust, and Bank of America.

In Japan the inter-war period produced a similar reduction in the number of banks, with the population of about 1,400 private banks in 1927 cut down to barely 400 ten years later. The Japanese banking crisis of 1927, together with strict bank regulations which followed, were probably the key to this change. Nevertheless, the reduction in the number of banks cleared the way for mergers such as the creation of the Sanwa Bank of Osaka in 1936. It also allowed the five big banks (Mitsui, Mitsubishi, Sumitomo, Yasuda and Dai-Ichi) to increase their share of Japan's bank deposits to 30 per cent by 1936.

For these very large banking enterprises the inter-war period was the opportunity to magnify their position and prestige in domestic markets. This opportunity was grasped in the ambitious expansion of branch banking. In Germany the major banks were operating only 153 branches in

In the twentieth century the large commercial banks were keen to commission new buildings which combined function with prestige. This perspective by Cyril Farey shows the ground floor interior of Midland Bank, London. Designed by Sir Edwin Lutyens in 1924, the banking hall featured verdite marble columns and a central light well. The result was described by A. S. G. Butler, Lutyens' biographer, as 'a palace of finance'.

Sir Edwin Lutyens, the eminent architect whose other achievements ranged from country houses to the Viceroy's House at New Delhi, designed four important buildings for Midland Bank between the wars. The headquarters at Poultry, London (seen here in a perspective by Cyril Farey, 1925) were designed by Lutyens in association with Gotch and Saunders and completed in stages between 1930 and 1939.

New and palatial buildings were commissioned by central banks and the major commercial banks throughout the world; the American and Canadian banks, in the view of one architectural critic, achieved 'a uniform temple standard' of building. The London clearing banks and the Hongkong and Shanghai Bank were similarly ambitious with their inter-war headquarters buildings. At local level this concern for a strong public image affected the design of branch buildings, and increasingly the commercial banks chose standardized styles and features for their new local offices.

The fine architectural clothing of the major banks also reflected the growing size and complexity of banking bureaucracy. The management of the large banks now required a more elaborate hierarchy of command, complete with all grades of staff from junior clerk to general manager. Moreover, the larger banks began to make much greater use of specialists in the inter-war period, instead of relying upon the all-round skills of their mainstream bankers. The management of premises and staff, legal expertise and economic intelligence were areas in which many banks now recognized the need for specialization.

Parallel to these trends in banking management, the 1920s and 1930s also saw real progress in systems of handling payments and record-keeping. Telephones and typewriters, calculating machines and addressing machines had, of course, made their banking début well before the First World War but this equipment was rarely found outside headquarters. Record-keeping in small banks and branch offices had been dominated by handwritten ledgers and registers of securities; the only mechanical aids were coin-weighing scales and the cumbersome hand-presses used for wet-copying manuscript documents. In the inter-war period, by contrast, banks in America and Europe introduced ledger-posting machines, dictaphones, loose-leaf binders and card-indexes not only at their head offices but at branches as well. The

John Dillinger, notorious as a bank robber in the United States in the 1920s and 30s. Organized crime remained a constant threat to the expansion of the banking system.

1913 but by 1929 that total had reached 698. In France the three giant commercial banks (the Crédit Lyonnais, Société Générale and Comptoir National d'Escompte) trebled the combined total of their branches from about 1,400 in 1914 to 3,500 in 1932. In the United Kingdom the same intensive development of branch banking – especially in suburban territory – lifted the 'Big Five's' total of branches from about 6,400 to 8,300 between 1920 and 1929.

The foremost commercial banks were enjoying a heyday in terms of style as well as sheer size. The ambitious bank architecture of the nineteenth and early twentieth centuries now turned to styling which was very grand indeed. Expenditure on bank headquarters was especially conspicuous.

The banking hall of the Union Trust building in Pittsburgh in the 1920s, featuring high-security counter grilles.

Mellon Bank, Pittsburgh. Designed as an office and shop complex by Frederick Osterling in 1917, this remarkable Gothic building was acquired in 1922 by the Union Trust company. Union Trust became part of the Pittsburgh-based Mellon Bank in 1946.

The City of London witnessed an unprecedented level of building activity between the wars. The head office of the Westminster Bank, Lothbury (now National Westminster Bank) was built between 1922 and 1931. The architects were Mewes and Davis.

The Madras office of the State Bank of India, an impressive adaptation of national styles and emblems for a large banking institution. The State Bank of India, which was established in 1955 as the successor to the Imperial Bank of India, now has over 5,000 branches in India.

The Osterreichische Postsparkasse, Vienna, designed by Otto Wagner in 1906. Wagner, leader of the Vienna school of architecture, employed a plain functional style which was entirely new to banking.

'Black Thursday' on Wall Street, New York, 24 October 1929. The Great Crash in security prices was not only a signal for recession but also the stimulus for restructuring the American banking system in the 1930s.

Mechanization also helped to strengthen the position of women in banking, as large numbers were recruited to operate the new machinery. This was certainly a factor in the rise of 2,000 in the number of women employed by the London clearing banks between 1929 and 1935, at a time when the total number of their male employees actually fell by 4,000.

In stark contrast to these signs of banking development, financial and political upheavals in the inter-war economy introduced severe strains and distortion in banking business. By the later 1920s it was already clear that the post-war surge in industrial activity could not be sustained. The leading economies carried a huge over-capacity of capital, stocks and employment, while speculation had fuelled rising share prices in the main financial centres. The reality of the position was finally brought home by the Wall Street crash of October 1929.

At the height of the crisis a group of senior American bankers had claimed to have halted the massive slide in share prices and established a $1 billion relief fund. When these claims did not prove meaningful, public sentiment in America turned against the banks. As the United States entered the years of slump – industrial production fell by one third and unemployment rose to about one quarter of the work-force between 1929 and 1933 – the banks in turn suffered a crisis of confidence. Between mid-1931 and the end of 1932, for instance, total banking deposits slumped from $51.8 billion to $41.6 billion. Of the 25,000 American banks open in 1929, no less than 1,350 banks were forced to close down in 1930, another 2,293 failed during 1931, and 1,453 went under in 1932. Further pandemonium followed when a run on the Michigan banks overspilled into New York and New Jersey, eventually forcing President Roosevelt to close the banks between 6 March and 13 March 1933. Using new emergency powers to investigate banking liquidity, the United States government then disqualified another

ledger-posting machines, in particular, reduced much of the routine manual work in recording payments and preparing statements of account. Even so, not all banks followed this trend. After a visit to an old-established European bank in the early 1930s, for instance, one British banker described it as:

> . . . living for all practical purposes well back in the last century. It works very cumbrously, improvements are taboo, and its only faint touch with mechanization is . . . the acquisition of a few typewriters, and that only very recently.

Five pound note issued by Fox Fowler and Co. of Wellington, Somerset, in 1921. In the long tradition of English country banking, the Wellington bank was the last private bank to issue its own notes until its acquisition by Lloyds Bank in 1921.

The skyscraper offices of the National City Bank-Farmers Trust Company, New York. From a postcard of the late 1930s.

2,100 banks from reopening.

The American banks were clearly under public scrutiny as well as under market pressures. Between 1932 and 1934 a Senate sub-committee closely examined the role of the banks in the securities market and, as a result, the United States Congress introduced new controls over the banking system. The Glass–Steagall Banking Act of 1934 (named after the chairmen of the committees of the Senate and the House of Representatives which steered through the legislation) was a broad-based and durable series of reforms. It awarded the Federal Reserve Bank greater powers of supervision and intervention, introduced a deposit insurance scheme to protect bank customers, and insisted that investment banking should be segregated from commercial banking. In the aftermath of this legislation many American private banks gave up their deposit-taking business. Others vested their securities business in new companies in which they were the main shareholders. The most prominent exam-

ple of this switch was J. P. Morgan & Co's transfer of its investment work to the new concern of Morgan Stanley & Co, while the original firm continued as a deposit bank.

In Europe the banking industry was also undergoing crisis and recession. Against the background of the reparations problem and the stockmarket crash of 1929, the political success of the Nazi party in the German elections of 1930 triggered a sudden withdrawal of foreign credits and deposits from German banks in 1930–1. The problem was compounded by the failure of the Creditanstalt, Austria's largest commercial bank, in May 1931. The Creditanstalt was eventually repaired and put back in action (partly as a result of intervention by the Bank of England), but in the meantime the German banks had suffered heavy withdrawals. International rescue proposals failed to stem the loss of confidence or to prevent the closure of such a prominent concern as the Danat-Bank in July 1931.

Only when Germany's creditors agreed to a series of moratoriums, or 'standstill'

Architectural splendour was not exclusive to city-centre banks. This photograph of 1937 shows the temple-like building of the First National Bank of Shawnestown, Illinois, USA.

Montagu Norman (later Lord Norman) in 1931. As Governor of the Bank of England between 1920 and 1944, Norman was a dominating – and highly individualistic – influence on central banking in the middle decades of the twentieth century.

Commerz- und Privat-Bank, and a 35 per cent share in the Deutsche Bank. The firm grip of nationalization was relaxed by the Reich's sale of its shares between 1933 and 1936, but in the interval the new German Banking Act of 1934 had introduced strict licensing and supervision rules. The Nazis' ideology of 'Aryanization' also changed the German banking scene by forcing private Jewish banks either to give up their business or to transfer their activities to new or retitled firms.

Banking in France and the United Kingdom was not thrown off balance so obviously as in America and Germany. Even so, the aftermath of the world crisis of 1929–30 was a tense period for the banking industry. In France the victims included the Banque Adam, a regional bank centred in Boulogne which suspended business in 1930, and the Banque Nationale de Crédit, which failed in the summer of 1931. In comparison, the British banks emerged from the crisis relatively unscathed. The merchant banks were hard hit by the outflow of deposits (especially foreign deposits) in 1931–2, whereas the clearing banks saw only a small dip of less than 5 per cent of their deposits. The main centre of crisis activity was the Bank of England's defence of the value of sterling in the summer of 1931, a campaign which owed much to the co-operation of the Federal Reserve Bank and the Banque de France.

If there was a single theme to banking experiments in these years of crisis and recession, it was the encroaching authority of government regulation. This change of emphasis was explicit in America (particularly through the Glass–Steagall Act) and in Germany. It was also implicit in the banking industry in France and the United Kingdom. The French government and the Banque de France were selective in the support which they gave during the years of crisis. While intervention saved the Banque de l'Union Parisienne in 1931, the Banque Nationale de Crédit was consigned to liquidation in the same year. Even in London, official policy was an increasingly promi-

agreements, in August 1931 did the situation return to any kind of normality, though the price paid by the international banking community was heavy. British banks, for example, opened credit facilities of about £65 million to German banks and other companies, but under the repeatedly renewed standstill arrangements less than half that amount had been repaid at the outbreak of the Second World War in 1939. It was not until 1961 that the last debts under the moratorium were repaid to British creditors.

The standstill deal had given the German government breathing space in which to force reconstruction upon the banking system. New measures included the injection of 1.25 billion marks in loans and new capital, and the merger of the Dresdner Bank with the remnants of the Danat-Bank, with the Reich owning two-thirds of the shares; the State also took a controlling share in the

The chandelier and octagonal ceiling of Daiwa Europe's entrance hall, King William Street, London. The original design, by J. M. and H. L. Anderson, was completed for the Phoenix Assurance Company in 1915.

The doorway of the Banque de France's Hotel Gaillard building, Paris. Thought to have been part of the royal chateau of Fontainbleau in the reign of Francis I, the doorway was acquired by the banker and collector Baron Emile Gaillard and incorporated into the new Hotel Gaillard between 1878 and 1884.

nent feature of the banking scene – not only in large monetary issues such as the abandonment of the gold standard in September 1931 and the conversion of war loans in 1932, but also through frequent intervention by the Treasury and the Bank of England in industrial and international finance. Indeed, the Bank of England was a prime mover in such initiatives as the Bankers' Industrial Development Company, formed in 1930 by the Bank and the major commercial banks to channel investment towards small and medium-sized industrial companies. Under the charismatic leadership of its Governor, Montagu Norman, the Bank was also embroiled in a series of company rescue operations. Suitable cases for treatment ranged from major industrial concerns such as Beardmore, the Glasgow shipbuilders, and the Lancashire Cotton Corporation to international groups such as the Anglo-South American Bank and the Royal Mail shipping group. London's merchant banks played a vital role in many of these reconstructions, and gained thereby influence and experience in the area of corporate finance.

The Second World War and the immediate post-war period immensely reinforced the connection between banking and official policy. In Germany the supply of war finance was well under way from the mid-1930s, largely through the massive increase in banknote circulation and the issue of short-term government bonds. Thereafter, the Reichsbank was tightly controlled by Hitler's regime, especially after Hjalmar Schacht and his co-directors were removed from office in January 1939. In the war years the British banks were subject to rigorous controls over foreign exchange, lending priorities and even opening hours. Banking business was switched almost entirely into government hands and by 1945 no less than 82 per cent of the deposits of the London clearing banks were in the form of government paper and cash. The banks were also active in the marketing and distribution of savings certificates and defence bonds.

As in the First World War, the banking industry within the combatant countries required radical adjustment to staffing and management. If the United Kingdom was typical, over 50 per cent of pre-war personnel had joined up by 1942, and inevitably the banks again turned to temporary staff and the recall of retired employees. Female staff, the numbers of whom had steadily increased in the 1920s and 1930s, were an indispensable part of maintaining services during the war, and by 1945 women occupied approximately two in every five posts in the European and American banks.

For at least five years after the war ended in 1945, the banking world remained at the call of government policy. At one level, official controls continued to affect foreign exchange movements, interest rates, and the pattern of lending. At a more mundane level, building restrictions held the banks back from restoring their wrecked or damaged property. In complete contrast to such passing adversities, the nationalization of the Banque de France in 1945 and the Bank of England in 1946 brought to an end a remarkable tradition in banking. For five centuries or more, institutions which were essentially private in ownership and constitution had acted as bankers for princes and governments, often at great risk to themselves. Until their change of status after the war, the central banks of England and France were the last of that extraordinary breed.

Above all, the international economy of the immediate post-war world was dominated by the American dollar. The dollar became the mid-twentieth century equivalent of gold values, with the United States economy and banking system having the capacity for American war finance and for a very large proportion of their allies' debts. The outcome was that by 1944 the United States was the lead hand in the settlement of the post-war financial scene. That hand was played in July 1944 at the Allies' finance conference in New Hampshire.

The Bretton Woods Conference, in which the British economist John Maynard

Keynes was a powerful influence, produced heroic and durable resolutions to the post-war economic confusion. The International Monetary Fund (IMF), based in Washington, was designed as a support for international trade and co-operation, mainly by setting rates of exchange but also by supplying credit to member states suffering balance-of-payments difficulties. The original $10 billion capital for these operations was supplied by the forty member states. Each member was also required to become a founder of the parallel International Bank for Reconstruction and Development (the World Bank), founded at the same time in Washington. The initial duties of the World Bank were to finance the rehabilitation of those countries most hurt by the war, but it quickly moved on to the support of development projects and other financial aid in the wider world.

These authoritative changes in the world financial scene introduced the hope of co-operation and international planning in the banking industry. Nevertheless, by 1950 these initiatives were not proven or tested in action. Many of the methods and characteristics of banking remained as before. Certainly the dollar and the American banking industry were in the ascendant, but the 'big battalions' which had dominated the banking scene since the early years of the twentieth century were still in the front row of public prestige and awareness. Stockmarket disaster, recession and war had modified though not defeated the expansive mood so characteristic of early twentieth-century banking.

CHAPTER FIVE

THE MODERN FACE OF BANKING

Banking in the later 20th century

For centuries the development of banking business has been tied to regions and phases of strong economic growth. On these terms the prospects for vigorous development after the Second World War looked grim, with most of the leading economies in a state of industrial and financial exhaustion. In the event, the quarter century which followed produced fast growth in output (at an annual rate of about 5 per cent in the main industrial nations) and relatively low rates of inflation and unemployment. A period which began in conditions of austerity had altered within two decades to an age of material affluence.

This recovery owed much to firm economic management and international co-operation. Never before had the world economic picture been so dominated by intervention, planning and regulation. The Bretton Woods agreements of 1944 had stabilized international monetary relationships. The Marshall Plan of 1948 provided $14 billion of American finance (mostly in grants) for reconstruction projects throughout Europe. Above all, the United States' conversion to liberalized non-tariff trade and the adoption of the General Agreement on Tariffs and Trade (GATT) in 1947 speeded up the recovery of industrial output in Europe and the Far East.

The role of banking in this post-war economic renaissance was bound to be influenced by official intervention, and banks throughout the world were indeed operating under a panoply of official instructions. These rules included credit restrictions, building regulations, foreign exchange controls and other legacies of war. They also included close supervision of banking in occupied countries. Hence, in Japan between 1945 and 1955 anti-trust legislation compelled the *zaibatsu* banks to break their links with industry and even change their names – the Yasuda Bank, for example, altered its name to Fuji Bank in 1948. In West Germany restrictions left the head offices of the major banks closed between 1945 and 1957–58 and placed their branches under the control of successor banks in the regions. It was only when the Allies ended these controls in 1957 that the Deutsche Bundesbank was established as a central bank along the lines of the Federal Reserve Bank, with the important addition of Bundesbank branches in the federal regions.

Perhaps the lasting feature of banking regulations after the war was the confinement of banks to particular types of business or geographical areas. In the United Kingdom this segmentation was traditional, with clearing banks, merchant banks and discount houses all occupying well-defined territory, but in America these distinctions were more recent. The Glass–Steagall Act of 1934 had insisted that American banks should opt for either deposit business or investment banking (see p. 116); savings and loans institutions were to fulfil a separate function by attracting long-term savings and providing loans for

Frankfurt-am-Main, West Germany, remains one of the dominant centres of world finance. The new Landeszentralbank in the Frankfurt banking quarter was designed by Jochem Jourdan and completed in 1987. Influences included Soane's designs for the Bank of England, and Wagner's Postparkasse, Vienna.

housing rather in the style of British building societies. Similarly in Japan, the Securities and Exchange Law of 1947 separated commercial and investment banking. Specialist banking business was directed to new institutions such as the People's Finance Corporation (1949) and the Housing Loan Corporation (1950).

Demarcation affected not only types of banking but also the national frontiers of business. Throughout the world, governments imposed limits or even bans on foreign ownership of banks; others forbade or made it difficult for overseas banks to open branches or to establish subsidiary banks. Some markets were entirely closed to Western banks. In the Eastern bloc and China, for example, the only remaining vehicle for business was the traditional 'correspondent' banking relationship, in which banks simply acted as their correspondent banks' agents in their own territories.

This vast array of regulations and barriers meant that in the post-war world banks were somewhat glued to their existing lines of business. At a time of generalized economic growth, this left them with little room for competition and expansion either at home or abroad, and to many modern bankers, the period from the end of the Second World War until 1970 may seem flat in performance and achievement when compared with the fast pace of change in the 1970s and 1980s. Yet those were years in which bankers successfully sought alternative means of generating income – by structural change, through new types of business, or by presenting themselves more directly to their customers.

Innovations in banking had been in short supply earlier in the twentieth century. Apart from the mechanization of bookkeeping (see p. 108), banks had edged towards a larger market by offering accounts for small savers, providing foreign exchange and trusteeship services, and by making greater use of press advertising. Shortly before the Second World War the American and Australian banks had also introduced the principle of personal loans, in which lending was related to an individual's ability to pay rather than to the security which he or she could offer. This approach, parallel to the formation of hire-purchase companies, was widely

Making money: the printing of dollar notes at the United States mint in Washington DC, USA. Dollar bills continue to bear the portrait of President George Washington, who had entrusted the management of United States' currency to the Treasury in 1789.

The Federal Reserve Board Building, Washington, designed by Marriner Eccles and completed in 1936. The 'Fed' has been the cornerstone of the American financial system since its creation in 1913.

adopted in the late 1950s and provided the platform for modern consumer finance. Such emphasis on the individual customer was naturally a factor in Western banks' entry into hire-purchase business in the late 1950s and 1960s.

Payments systems were also the subject of experiment and innovation in the period just after the war. The 'Charg-It' system launched by the Flatbush National Bank, New York, in 1946 was the forerunner of the modern bank card by combining consumer credit with a cashless method of payment. The system was quickly adapted by Diners Club and American Express, and by the mid-1950s about 100 American banks were supplying a credit card service. European banks did not take this route until the later 1960s, but from the 1970s the popularity and effectiveness of bank card products enormously increased throughout the world. Initially most of these products were demarcated, with separate cards for cheque

identification, consumer credit, and automatic cash-dispensers. By the 1980s, however, commercial banks were collaborating to offer commonly accepted 'brand' cards with a wide range of facilities. The evolution of the bank card in the post-war period was also closely linked to the banks' growing investment in electronic transfers of payments and charges.

Probably the most significant innovation of the immediate post-war banking scene was the creation of the Eurodollar or Euromoney market in the early 1950s. The spur was the unwillingness of European banks (including Russian and Eastern-bloc banks) to leave dollar deposits with American banks. United States regulations in effect made it unprofitable for the Europeans to place their dollar business with American banks: consequently European banks (and some non-banking institutions) built up a market for themselves in dollar-denominated credits – borrowing and lending to

Experiments in retail banking: this drive-in bank was opened in Hollywood, California, in 1951.

For more than three hundred years the counting of bank notes has been a familiar but demanding part of banking routine. As this cashier in a Qatari bank demonstrates, this is an area where machines and electronics are only a limited help.

The National Commercial Bank, Jeddah, Saudi Arabia. Middle Eastern institutions have emerged as a significant force in international markets, especially since the early 1970s.

and Union Bank of Switzerland – played a leading role in these markets, channelling large private funds into the international markets. Eurodollar business was also an incentive for the Swiss banks to enlarge their branch networks outside Europe. This international prominence, together with the continuing inflow of private and corporate funds into Swiss accounts, gave the bankers of Switzerland a distinctive influence and reputation between the 1950s and 1970s. It was their impact on the foreign exchange markets which earned them the sobriquet 'gnomes of Zurich' during the sterling crisis of 1964 – a tag which became part of press vocabulary but misunderstood the new stature of Swiss banking in the currency markets.

Even if Swiss and German banks were commonly the major participants, the overwhelming majority of Eurodollar deals were transacted on the London market. An important aspect of the London Eurodollar market was the issue of dollar-denominated industrial bonds, or 'Eurobonds'. This business was pioneered by the small but innovative merchant bank of S. G. Warburg, which launched the first Eurobond

In recent years surveillance by video cameras has contributed to greater security in branch banks. This attempted armed robbery at a bank in California, USA, was fully recorded on video tape in 1985.

adjust their liquidity position. The expansion of the market was extremely rapid, with a total valuation of about $9 billion in 1964 rising to $46 billion in 1970 and $220 billion net in 1975.

The major Swiss banks – notably the Swiss Credit Bank, Swiss Bank Corporation

The proliferation of cash dispensing machines has transformed personal banking in the 1970s and 1980s, giving customers a round-the-clock service. This early-morning photograph shows Midland Bank's branch at Keswick, Cumbria.

'A more magnificent banking hall is not likely to be found in Switzerland.' The Zurich office of the Swiss Bank Corporation, built in 1898 and featuring a statue of Helvetia by Richard Kissling. The building was demolished in 1956.

loan for Autostrade Italiane in 1963. Sieg-mund Warburg, coming from the distin-guished family of Hamburg bankers and having served his apprenticeship with the London Rothschilds, was one of the out-standing banking personalities of the post-war period. His other achievements included the capture of valuable business in corporate finance, particularly in merg-ers and acquisitions. Warburg's aggressive style during the 'Aluminium War' of 1958–9 produced victory for his clients, Reynolds of America and the British group Tube Investments, in their bid for British Aluminium; that style also showed that a merchant bank could sidestep the wishes of the Bank of England and the UK Treasury.

Structural change provided a means by which it was possible for major banks to overcome local and international restric-tions. In the United States the New York banks began a new round of amalgama-tions soon after the Second World War. These started with the Bank of New York's purchase of the Fifth Avenue Bank in 1948, and culminated in 1955, when the National City Bank amalgamated with its old rival the First National Bank to form the First National City Bank, while the Chase National Bank and the Bank of Manhattan together formed the Chase Manhattan Bank. These two giants, along with the Bank of America in San Francisco, now occupied the first three places in the top

Marble, wood and leather – traditional features of
bank interiors in a modern setting at the National
Bank of Georgia, Atlanta.

league of world banking.

Amalgamations also altered the post-war banking scene in France. In 1945 the republic had nationalized not only the Banque de France but also the four largest commercial banks (the Crédit Lyonnais, Société Générale, Comptoir d'Escompte, and the Banque Nationale pour le Commerce et l'Industrie). The change of ownership did not radically alter the management and business of these world-ranking concerns, but in a highly regulated market they used amalgamations and alliances to defend and enlarge their business. The most ambitious of these mergers was the amalgamation in 1966 of Comptoir National d'Escompte and the Banque Nationale to form the Banque

Nationale de Paris. The new combination emerged as the largest of the French banks and only slightly behind the three largest American banks in the world league.

In the United Kingdom the 1918 agreements between the government and banks – in which the banks had undertaken to consult the Treasury over amalgamation plans – had proved remarkably durable. The first sign of any relaxation was the Bank of England's permission for the National Provincial Bank to purchase the District Bank in 1962. Five years later a report by the Prices and Incomes Board, indicating that the Treasury and Bank of England 'would not obstruct some further mergers', was the green light for a remark-

18 Pine Street, New York, the headquarters of the Chase National Bank between 1928 and 1955 and subsequently the head office of Chase Manhattan Bank.

Corporate art in the 1970s: Jean Dubuffet's *Four Trees* on the Chase Manhattan Plaza, New York.

able burst of merger negotiations. The creation of the National Westminster Bank in 1968, by an amalgamation of the Westminster Bank with the National Provincial, produced the fifth largest bank in the world; a plan to merge Barclays, Lloyds and Martins in the same year promised to create an even larger concern, with as much as 45 per cent of the business of the London clearing banks. It was at this point that the authorities' instincts for regulation reasserted themselves; the Monopolies Commission disallowed the Barclays-Lloyds-Martins plan but did not object to Barclays' acquisition of Martins in 1968.

Structural change was also used to extend the existing overseas business of the major banks and to overcome the barriers which still affected international banking. In some cases, amalgamations gave international banks a wider geographical scope. For example, the merger of the Standard Bank of South Africa with the Bank of West Africa in 1966 created a pan-African bank; when the Standard amalgamated with the Chartered Bank of India, Australia and China five years later, the Standard Chartered group became a strong contender in Eastern banking. The Hongkong and Shanghai Banking Corporation had also developed a larger range of business through its acquisition of the Mercantile Bank in 1959, the British Bank of the Middle East in 1960, and a controlling interest in

The headquarters of Fourth Financial, Wichita, Kansas, featuring a giant mobile by Alexander Calder in the entrance hall.

Marine Midland Bank in 1980

The Treaty of Rome of 1957, which set the agenda for the European Economic Community or 'Common Market', was clearly another opportunity (and a challenge) for the banking industry. The European banks responded in the 1960s with a network of alliances and agreements, their purpose being to share in joint ventures and jointly-owned subsidiaries which could bid for large-scale projects in international banking. An early example was the European Advisory Committee, formed in 1963 by Deutsche Bank, Amsterdam Rotterdam Bank, Midland Bank and Société Générale of Belgium. Out of this grouping emerged a series of joint banking ventures in Europe and America and, in 1970, the Brussels-based European Banks International Company (EBIC). A similar group, 'the Club of Three,' was brought together the same year by the Crédit Lyonnais, Commerzbank, and Banco di Roma, and in 1971 the Dresdner Bank, Bayerische Hypotheken-

und Wechselbank, Banque de Bruxelles and Algemeene Nederland entered a co-operation arrangement.

This proliferation of co-operation in banking was a genuine effort to cross the frontiers of national markets and, at heart, to move towards integrated European and global banking. Similar initiatives in central banking were actually delayed for another twenty years, until the movement towards an integrated European market (with 1992 as the target date) forced the financial community to consider some form of supra-national banking authority. By the late 1980s a sub-group of the Committee of Central Bank Governors was investigating options for a European central bank, the creation of a uniform European currency, and the operation of a central monetary policy. This sub-group, known as the 'Delors Committee' after its instigator Jacques Delors, was faced with a long menu of competing ideas on banking integration. The French, for example, sought the expan-

The hanging signs in Lombard Street are reminders of the goldsmith origins of many London banks. The shop signs were banned by Charles II as being too dangerous but they were reinstated to celebrate the coronation of King Edward VII in 1902. The 'King's Head' was adopted by the Canadian Bank of Commerce and the 'Cat-a-Fiddling' by the Commercial Bank of Scotland.

sion of existing European institutions to take on a central banking role, while the German preference was for a new European central bank which (like their own Bundesbank) would enjoy guaranteed independence from official controls. In early 1989 the outcome of the Committee's work was still not known but it was certain none the less that integration in Europe would require more deliberate co-operation between central banks and other regulators of banking.

Most of these initiatives from the 1960s to the late 1980s affected only the major institutions in the banking world. Co-operation was confined mainly to the largest deposit-taking banks and (latterly) the central banks. There was relatively little interchange and co-operation between deposit banks and merchant banks, and there were no obvious attempts to break down the distinctions between banking and other types of financial services.

From the early 1970s, however, the banking industry was given much greater incentive – even compulsion – to climb over the barriers between different types of business. The orderly markets and managed economies of the post-war world came under increasing pressure from inflation and from the trade deficits incurred by the United States during the Vietnam War. Then, in 1971, the international monetary stability inherited from the Bretton Woods agreement came to a sudden end. American gold reserves tumbled and devaluation of the dollar seemed inevitable. President Nixon suspended the US Treasury's undertaking to convert foreign banks' dollars into gold, with the result that exchange rates throughout the Western world were allowed to 'float'. New agreements on exchange rates in December 1971 were much looser than their 1944 counterparts, and the crisis left the Japanese yen and German mark riding at much higher values against the US dollar.

In the wake of the 1971 crisis, the international banks were free to compete vigorously for Eurodollar business. That business, centred on London, became even more hectic when the first 'oil shock' of 1973 produced a massive inflow of deposits from the oil-rich countries of the Organization of Petroleum Exporting Countries (OPEC). Scores of banks were anxious to share the fruits of the burgeoning Euromarkets. Already, over 240 foreign banks were represented in London, and the large contingent from America was especially active, preferring the high growth rates to be obtained from international business to their highly regulated home market. In the years after the 1973 oil shock, for example, the largest American banks were generating more than three-quarters of their profits from international business.

This turbulent period was also the heyday of recycling 'petrodollars'. Dollar funds deposited by oil-producing countries were recycled on to the credit-hungry developing countries, especially in Latin America. With little or no regulation on the level of lending and investment, this phase of international banking was to have a profound influence on the financial scene later in the century (see p. 145).

The opening up of domestic banking, though not so rapid as in international business, was also underway from the early 1970s. Inflation was a key influence, especially in so far as it permitted newcomers and non-banking concerns to exploit the gap between inflation rates and bank interest rates. In the United Kingdom the Bank of England's 'Competition and Credit Control' policy statement of September 1971 enabled the British commercial banks to respond, for lending restrictions were removed and the banks were allowed to compete for business in the wholesale money markets; they also showed a much greater interest in diversification, and in the early 1970s their subsidiaries included unit trusts, insurance brokers, merchant banks, and travel interests.

In the United States during the period of high inflation, the banks faced strong competition from firms which were not regulated in the same way and could afford to

The banking hall of the Coast Savings Bank, Los Angeles, USA. This design, conveying the traditional banking image of solidity and security, was the work of the architects Kohn Pederson Fox Company.

The headquarters of Coast Savings, Los Angeles, USA, designed by Kohn Pederson Fox Conway.

offer high rates of interest to savers. Some foreign banks, for instance, had greater freedom to open branch banks across State boundaries than their American counterparts. The International Banking Act of 1978 evened up this position. By then, however, United States policy was *en route* to deregulation in its financial markets.

In 1975 the New York Stock Exchange ended its ancient tradition of fixed commissions and allowed firms outside the Exchange to enter the securities markets. With the help of giant strides in information technology, this revolution allowed financial institutions to roll together stockbroking, investment management, and deposit banking for its customers. Merrill Lynch's Cash Management Account, launched in the late 1970s, was a pioneer of this integrated form of finance. Other securities houses such as Salomon, Goldman Sachs and Shearson Lehmann also crossed over into the banking markets. Initially the deposit banks were slow to respond, and the Bank of America's purchase of a discount broker was the exception rather than the rule. By the late 1980s, however, the other barriers between types of banking business were also being dismantled. Early in 1989 the Federal Reserve reached the historic decision to allow commercial banks (such as Citicorp, Chase Manhattan and Security Pacific) to enter the investment banking business dominated by the likes of Morgan Stanley and Salomon Brothers. This deregulation was not absolute, as commercial banks were still required to concentrate their main resources on traditional banking, but it did signal the end of the remarkable 55-year reign of the Glass–Steagall Act (see p. 116).

When stockmarkets were deregulated in Canada in 1983, Australia in 1984 and, above all, in London in 1986, the banks were much more ready to enter new territory. Deregulation in the London market in October 1986, popularly known as the 'Big Bang', was neither a local nor an isolated event. It was preceded by a large and complex wave of takeovers and mergers involv-

The financial centre of Hong Kong featuring on the left of centre the new headquarters of the Hongkong and Shanghai Banking Corporation, (see also p.79).

The World Financial Center, Manhattan, New York, USA. This ambitious project by Cesar Pelli Associates was developed by Olympia and York and completed in 1988. The glass-topped Winter Garden was intended for public arts events and has seats for an audience of 2,000.

ing British stockbrokers or stockjobbers and international banks and securities houses. Full outside ownership of brokers and jobbers was permitted in the run-up to Big Bang; in that interval the new owners of stockbrokers included the Union Bank of Switzerland, which acquired Philips & Drew, Citicorp (Scrimgeour Vickers), and Shearson Lehmann (L. Messel). British banks were also in the hunt, with the merchant bank S. G. Warburg acquiring the brokers Mullens, and Rowe & Pitman, and clearing banks such as Barclays and the Midland taking over broking firms through the agency of their merchant bank subsidiaries. Even though London securities business still remained smaller in volume than its New York and Tokyo counterparts, the London banking market emerged as unquestionably the most international of the main financial centres. By the mid-1980s London was host to 400 foreign banks.

The banking world's journey towards deregulation was extremely bumpy. By the end of the 1980s, moreover, it was not obvious whether the journey had been completed, whether it was still in progress, or whether it had been re-routed. In domestic banking, the leading economies met a number of nasty surprises when their banks strayed into new territory. For example, the United Kingdom's 'Competition and Credit Control' policy produced unforeseen results by fuelling the growth of the 'secondary' banks, all lending heavily to the property sector. That bubble burst when in mid-1973 very high interest rates left many secondary banks in serious cash-flow difficulties. A chain reaction of collapse followed, beginning with the failure of London and County Securities in November 1973, and by the end of that year the exposure of twenty secondary banks had reached some £260 million. Prompt and decisive action by the Bank of England headed off the crisis, mainly through the launch of a 'lifeboat' operation. This initiative gathered together loans and guarantees from the Bank and from the clearing banks – support which reached nearly

£1,200 million by the end of 1974. Over the next seven years that commitment was gradually reduced as the secondary banks were either reconstructed or liquidated.

During the secondary banking crisis in the United Kingdom, the role of the central bank had been pivotal. Its actions were in a long tradition of co-operation within the British banking community, stretching back to the early nineteenth century. The old preference for regulation and supervision was also reasserted, particularly in the shape of the 1976 Banking Act. This

Modern outposts of banking: the Antarctic Station branch of the Banco de Credito e Inversiones, Chile.

Mobile banking: for more than 40 years the Scottish banks have provided travelling bank facilities for remote areas of the Highlands and Islands. This mobile bank of the Royal Bank of Scotland (which has more than 20 such vehicles) is staffed by Gaelic-speaking officials.

gave the Bank of England new powers of surveillance over the banking system and established a protection fund for bank depositors. It was even prepared to accept the responsibility of direct ownership of a banking unit, should the banking system appear to be threatened by the troubles of that bank. When in 1984 it became clear that Johnson Matthey bankers (JMB) was hopelessly overcommitted in trade finance the Bank bought JMB from the parent Johnson Matthey Corporation and arranged for the Bank and leading commercial banks to provide an indemnity of £150 million against JMB's losses. A 'domino-effect' series of crises was averted and all money drawn under the 1984 indemnity was eventually repaid by 1988.

The banking authorities in the other major economies also showed that they were prepared to intervene in domestic banking crises. This last-ditch rescue role was taken on by a government agency in more than one crisis of American banking in the 1980s. The Federal Deposit Insurance Corporation (FDIC), established under the terms of the Glass–Steagall Act in 1934, was primarily concerned with protecting bank depositors against loss from bank failure. However, after the collapse of the Continental Illinois banking group in 1984, the FDIC also took on the work of refunding the remains. The net cost of that operation was $1.7 billion. Four years later the FDIC was also prominent in the rescue of First Republic Bank, the largest bank in Texas.

International banking, too, suffered a full share of upsets when exchange rates were abandoned after 1971. Initially, those difficulties centred on foreign exchange losses in 1973–4. Even the Swiss banks, with their long tradition of security and stability, were forced to declare losses on foreign exchange business. Other banks could not survive such losses. In May 1974, despite an injection of $1 billion from the FDIC, the Franklin National Bank of New York failed; one month later the West German Herstatt bank closed its doors after suffering exchange losses of about $500 million. In

this climate it was vital that the European central banks should restore confidence in the currency markets. In West Germany the Bundesbank revised credit regulations and the banks' guarantee system, while foreign exchange speculation was curtailed. Similar disciplines were introduced by the Swiss authorities. In the United Kingdom the Bank of England asked for – and obtained – assurances from foreign banks that they would give full support to their London-based subsidiaries, branches and consortium ventures. These interventions had restored some calm to the banking scene by the mid-1970s.

Serious though the failures were, they paled in comparison with the problem posed by sovereign debt in the 1980s. After the first oil shock of 1973, the recycling of 'petrodollars' had led to huge loans and investments by the international banks (often with their governments' encouragement) in the less developed countries of Latin America and the Third World. This switch of funds was inspired by the idea that nation-states were safe from bankruptcy – a notion that ignored one of the main themes of banking history. In 1982, however, the Mexican government duly announced that it was unable to meet payments on its $100 billion foreign debt. The news triggered a world-wide debt crisis in which banks were forced to calculate the cost of actual and potential defaults by sovereign debtors. In many cases the debts were rescheduled or renegotiated, but even so the sum of debt remained at a staggering level. The World Bank estimated that by 1988 the total debt of the less developed countries remained at $1,245 billion. But already, from the mid-1980s, most of the American and European banks had been writing off part of their Third World loans as bad debts, even if that meant declaring large losses in their annual accounts.

The risks and setbacks of international banking meant that by the late 1980s some of the ambitious plans for expansion drawn up in the 1970s were being abandoned or modified. Similarly, when the world-wide

stockmarket crash of October 1987 broke into the brave new world of deregulation, many banks pulled out of new areas of business or chose to develop 'niches' in the financial markets rather than pretend that they were global in the scope of their business. In London's International Stock Exchange many of those banks which had bought stockbroking firms in the run-up to Big Bang closed or cut back upon their securities operations in 1988 and 1989. In contrast, banks which had insisted on internal development of their securities business proved relatively successful in the deregulated markets.

By the end of the 1980s the major players on the banking scene were undoubtedly those which were represented in all the main financial centres and based upon a thriving home market. The supremacy of the Japanese banks in the top league of the world's banks (Table 4) reflected these strengths, and was a vivid reminder of the high value of the Japanese yen against the American dollar and the pound sterling. Whereas only one Japanese bank had featured amongst the largest ten banks in the world (ranked by total assets) in 1980, by 1987 no less than eight of the ten leaders were Japanese.

Massive as their resources were, these leading banks were only a minority in the population of the world's banks. By the late 1980s no less than 2,500 banks were listed as 'principal banks' in the authoritative *Bankers' Almanac*: the majority were deposit banks in origin, but the total also included central banks, merchant banks, investment houses and a host of other banking intermediaries. The global total was of course even higher: with the inclusion of regional and local banks, the population probably exceeded 20,000. But throughout the banking world there was now a strong challenge from non-banking financial companies. As the barriers between different types of business were lowered, the traditional territory occupied by the banks became the legitimate target for mortgage companies (the savings and loan institutions in the United

States and the building societies in Britain), unit trusts, insurance companies and even major retailing concerns such as Sears Roebuck, General Electric Credit, and Marks and Spencer. Often this competition was not sited on a 'level playing field', since the incoming institutions were not always affected by the supervision and taxation applied to deposit banking. By the later 1980s financial authorities world wide were under pressure to remove these anomalies and distortions in financial markets.

The counterpart to this increase in competition was the banking industry's greater freedom to compete for other types of financial business. Diversification and innovation were key factors in banking change throughout the 1970s and 1980s. Information technology clearly contributed to the process – new financial products, such as foreign exchange and interest swaps, proliferated at a rate which would have been impossible without the modern armoury of computer and communications equipment. In the run-up to Big Bang in the London market, for instance, a new high-technology trading floor could cost between ten and twenty million dollars, excluding the fabulous rewards paid to specialist dealers, yet for those banks who were prepared to compete there was little

A skyscraper view of the financial centre of Tokyo. In terms of the sheer size of their balance sheets, Japanese banks in Tokyo, Osaka, and Kobe dominated the top ranks of the world's financial institutions by the late 1980s.

(See previous spread) Perhaps the most celebrated bank building of modern times, the new headquarters of the Hongkong and Shanghai Banking Corporation (centre) was commissioned in 1979 and completed in 1985. Designed by Norman Foster, the emphasis throughout is high technology in building materials and banking systems.

option but to invest in top quality technology. Equally important, however, were changes in attitude to the sale of services. Where once banking had been perceived in a passive role – leaving it to the customer to make the first approach – by the third quarter of the twentieth century the industry was as aggressive as any other in the marketing of its products. This cultural change affected all types of banking business, from international and corporate business to local banking for personal customers. In all of these areas the emphasis switched to the creation, and heavy advertising, of new services or 'brands', while inside the banks the performance of management and staff was set against specific business targets.

The result of these fast technical and cultural changes was the transformation of banking from an industry with a narrow range of services to a business with a huge choice of products and facilities. Central banks, whose original role had been confined to the issue of state loans and currency, had emerged in the twentieth century as powerful influences on monetary and industrial policy, including the supervision of financial operations outside traditional banking. Merchant banking had become similarly broad in scope, with investment banking, corporate finance and other skills supplementing their expertise in international trade and finance.

The process of diversification was probably most obvious in the area of commercial banking. The banks had originally been limited to taking deposits, providing credit and offering a payments service to their customers. By the 1980s the banks were active in insurance, investment and securities, mortgage business, trade finance, venture capital, travel and an extraordinary range of advisory and consultancy work. In these activities it was appropriate that the retailing approach should be so prominent; the variety of services on offer was now closer to the world of the department store than to that of the specialist local business.

The banking industry is rightly proud of its heritage. Certainly there have been crises and setbacks in the long march of banking, yet towards the end of the twentieth century it is striking that so many of the great and familiar names have a deep-rooted pedigree. That pedigree has been earned not by following a single narrow path of business but by adapting to gradual or sudden shifts in the market-place. In this sense it is inconceivable that the banking business of fifty years ago or even twenty years ago, if transplanted into the late 1980s, could offer a meaningful service in the competitive markets of modern banking.

The ability and the will to adapt are quintessential to late twentieth-century banking. In part, the diversification of banking in the last two decades is the outcome of intense competition and structural change within the industry, but above all, the proliferation of services reflects the growing sophistication and complex needs of the banks' customers. Until the later nineteenth century banking served a relatively narrow section of the community. Important though that market may have been – especially in the finance of princes and governments – it is only in the last hundred years that the banking habit has become a commonplace of economic life. In the course of the twentieth century, the traditional large users of bank services have been joined by all types and sizes of customers expecting a high standard of service and security.

Expectations have been heightened as customers have taken a more analytical and demanding approach to their financial affairs. In the business sector, financial directors and treasurers have demanded flexibility and rapid response from their banks, while private customers have looked to their banks for professional efficiency and multi-purpose financial services. The innovations and diversity of the modern banking world are a response to those needs, echoing the close dialogue between banking and economic development for more than five centuries.

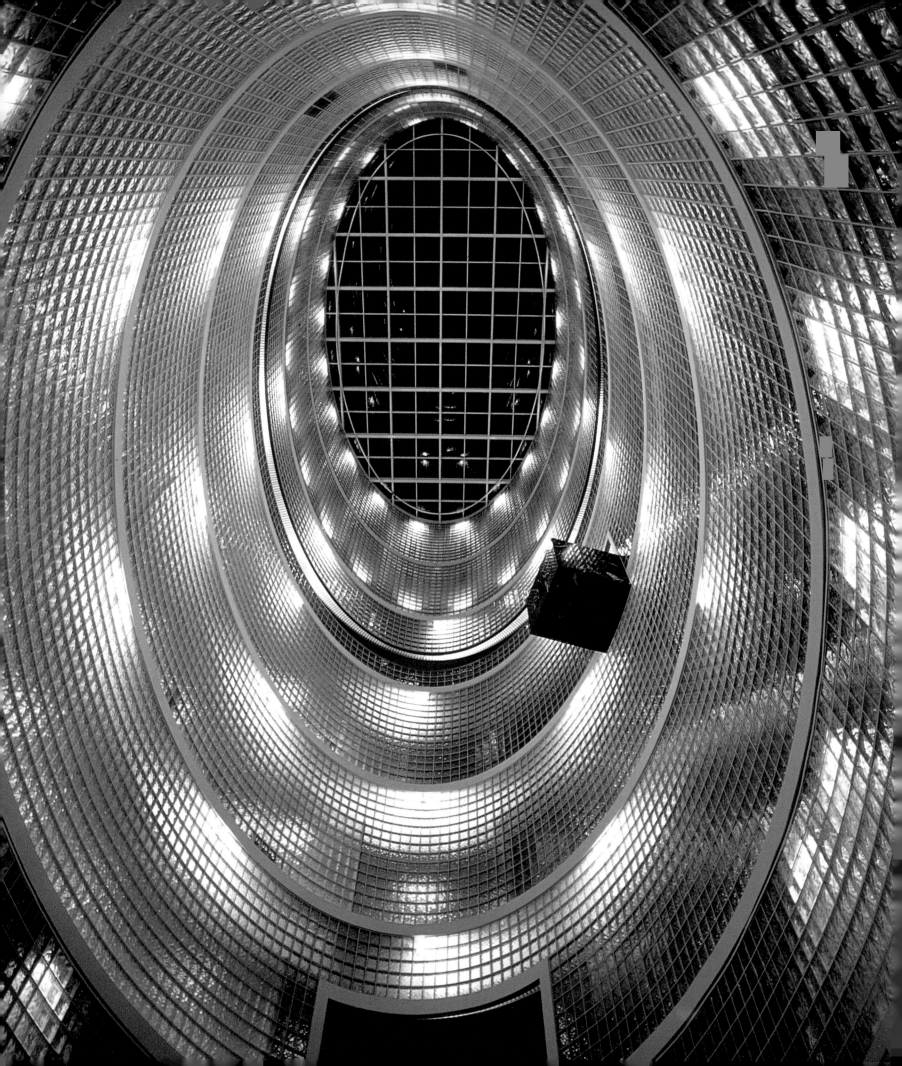

The headquarters of the Banco de Credito del Peru, Lima, Peru. This bank had been founded by Italian investors in 1889. The new reflective glass office was designed by Arquitectonica.

Part of the spectacular interior of the Banco de Credito, Lima, Peru.

TABLES

Table 1 *Summary balance sheet of the Medici at Florence, Rome and Venice, 1427*

Category		000 Florins	% of total
Liabilities			
Capital and undistributed profits		41	13.0
Current and deposit accounts	188		
Medici companies & partners	55		
	243	243	77.2
Correspondents		18	5.7
Trade debts		7	2.2
Other liabilities		6	1.9
Total liabilities		315	100
Assets			
Cash		16	5.1
Advances	105		
Medici companies & partners	92		
	197	197	62.6
Correspondents		65	20.6
Trade credits		12	3.8
Other assets		25	7.9
Total assets		315	100

Source: R. de Roover, *The Rise and Decline of the Medici Bank, 1397–1494* (Harvard University Press, 1963) pp. 206–47

Table 2 *Summary balance sheet of the Amsterdam Wisselbank, 1610–1700*

Date	Liabilities (million florins)			Assets (million florins)				
	Deposits	Accumulated profits	Total	Cash	City of Amsterdam	East India Co	Others	Total
1610	0.93	—	0.93	0.93	—	—	—	0.93
1620	1.94	0.15	2.09	1.86	—	0.10	0.13	2.09
1630	4.17	0.58	4.75	3.11	0.17	0.45	1.02	4.75
1640	8.08	1.17	9.25	5.82	—	—	3.43	9.25
1650	10.76	1.52	12.28	10.59	0.70	0.35	0.64	12.28
1660	7.60	1.57	9.17	6.85	1.83	—	0.49	9.17
1670	5.37	1.83	7.20	4.84	2.07	—	0.29	7.20
1680	7.95	2.18	10.13	6.16	2.07	1.61	0.29	10.13
1690	12.60	0.38	12.98	11.74	0.81	—	0.43	12.98
1700	16.28	0.60	16.88	13.37	2.38	0.50	0.63	16.88

Source: R.W. Goldsmith, *Premodern Financial Systems. A Historical Comparative Study* (Cambridge University Press, 1987) p. 216

Table 3 *Ranking of major commercial banks, 1908*

Bank	Deposits (£m)	Rank	Assets (£m)	Rank
Lloyds Bank	73	1	81	3
Crédit Lyonnais	69	2	92	2
Deutsche Bank	63	3	94	1
National Provincial Bank	57	4	63	6
[London City &] Midland Bank	56	5	66	5
National City Bank, New York	53	6	66	4
Société Générale	47	7	59	7
Barclay & Co	47	8	52	9
London & County Bank	46	9	55	8
National Bank of Commerce, New York	39	10	50	13
Comptoir National d'Escompte	39	11	52	10
Union of London & Smiths Bank	36	12	45	14
Capital & Counties Bank	35	13	38	15
Parr's Bank	29	14	35	17
Bank of Montreal	29	15	34	18
[London &] Westminster Bank	28	16	34	19
Dresdner Bank	27	17	51	12
Bank of New South Wales	27	18	36	16
Hongkong & Shanghai Banking Corporation	27	19	33	20
London & River Plate Bank	23	20	28	—
Banca Commerciale Italiana	19	—	51	11

Table 4 *Ranking of major commercial banks, 1987*

Bank	Deposits ($bn)	Rank	Assets Rank
Dai-Ichi Kangyo Bank, Tokyo	275	1	1
Sumitomo Bank, Osaka	258	2	2
Fuji Bank, Tokyo	249	3	3
Mitsubishi Bank, Tokyo	242	4	4
Sanwa Bank, Osaka	238	5	5
Norinchukin Bank, Tokyo	210	6	7
Industrial Bank of Japan, Tokyo	206	7	6
Mitsubishi Trust & Banking Corp, Tokyo	175	8	11
Tokai Bank, Nagoya	167	9	9
Sumitomo Trust & Banking Corp, Tokyo	159	10	13
Deutsche Bank, Frankfurt	155	11	15
Crédit Agricole Mutuel, Paris	151	12	8
Banque Nationale de Paris	150	13	12
Mitsui Bank, Tokyo	149	14	10
Mitsui Trust & Banking Co, Tokyo	149	15	14
National Westminster Bank, London	144	16	20
Crédit Lyonnais, Paris	142	17	16
Long Term Credit Bank of Japan, Tokyo	142	18	17
Barclays Bank, London	139	19	18
Taiyo Kobe Bank, Kobe	129	20	19

Source: American Banker (July 1988)

The massive scale of modern bank building projects is illustrated by this photograph of the banking hall of the Third National Bankl of Nashville, Tennessee, USA. The project was designed by Kohn Pederson Fox Company.

FURTHER READING

This short history has been based upon the growing literature of banking history. That literature is primarily in the form of company histories of individual banks, but over the last fifty years banking history has also been the subject of serious comparative study. The author is grateful to that international brigade of historians of business and banking. Other vital sources for the history of banking include the consistently high-quality journals of banking: for about 150 years publications such as the *Bankers' Magazine* (now *Banking World*), *The Economist*, *The Financial Times*, *The Banker*, and *The American Banker* have offered the historian great riches in comment and information.

The following suggestions for further reading are recently-published results of contemporary research on banking history:

Born, K. E., (translated V. R. Berghahn), *International Banking in the 19th and 20th Centuries*, Berg Publishers, Leamington, 1983

Channon, D. F., *British Banking Strategy and the International Challenge*, Macmillan, London, 1977

Chapman, S. D., *The Rise of Merchant Banking*, George Allen & Unwin, London, 1984

Collins, M., *Money and Banking in the UK. A History*, Croom Helm, London, 1988

Goldsmith, R. W., *Premodern Financial Systems. A Historical Comparative Study*, Cambridge University Press, Cambridge, 1987

Melton, F. T., *Sir Robert Clayton and the Origins of English Deposit Banking, 1658–1685*, Cambridge University Press, Cambridge, 1986

Parker, G., *The Emergence of Modern Finance in Europe 1500–1730*, Fontana, London, 1973

Price, K., *The Global Financial Village*, Banking World, London, 1986

Spooner, F. C., *The International Economy and Monetary Movements in France, 1493–1725*, Harvard University Press, Cambridge, Mass., 1972

INDEX

Safe-keeping: the entrance door to the Safe Deposit at Midland Bank's head office, London. The 25-ton steel door was built by the Chatwood Safe Company and had been displayed at the British Empire Exhibition in 1924.

Gold bullion and coin: after more than five centuries of public and commercial banking, trading in gold and silver still occupies an important corner of international financial markets.